BEHAVING

TO

BELONGING

ASCD MEMBER BOOK

Many ASCD members received this book as a
member benefit upon its initial release.

Learn more at: **www.ascd.org/memberbooks**

FROM
BEHAVING
TO
BELONGING

· · · · · · ·

The Inclusive Art of Supporting Students Who Challenge Us

Julie CAUSTON
Kate MACLEOD

ASCD | Alexandria, Virginia USA

1703 N. Beauregard St. • Alexandria, VA 22311-1714 USA
Phone: 800-933-2723 or 703-578-9600 • Fax: 703-575-5400
Website: www.ascd.org • E-mail: member@ascd.org
Author guidelines: www.ascd.org/write

Ranjit Sidhu, *CEO and Executive Director;* Stefani Roth, *Publisher;* Genny Ostertag, *Director, Content Acquisitions;* Julie Houtz, *Director, Book Editing & Production;* Jamie Greene, *Editor;* Judi Connelly, *Senior Art Director;* Donald Ely, *Associate Art Director;* Kelly Marshall, *Manager, Production Services;* Circle Graphics, *Typesetter;* Trinay Blake, *E-Publishing Specialist*

All web links in this book are correct as of the publication date below but may have become inactive or otherwise modified since that time. If you notice a deactivated or changed link, please e-mail books@ascd.org with the words "Link Update" in the subject line. In your message, please specify the web link, the book title, and the page number on which the link appears.

PAPERBACK ISBN: 978-1-4166-2929-0   ASCD product #121011
PDF E-BOOK ISBN: 978-1-4166-2931-3; see Books in Print for other formats.
Quantity discounts are available; e-mail programteam@ascd.org or call 800-933-2723, ext. 5773, or 703-575-5773. For desk copies, go to www.ascd.org/deskcopy.

ASCD Member Book No. FY20-8 (Jul. 2020). ASCD Member Books mail to Premium (P), Select (S), and Institutional Plus (I+) members on this schedule: Jan, PSI+; Feb, P; Apr, PSI+; May, P; Jul, PSI+; Aug, P; Sep, PSI+; Nov, PSI+; Dec, P. For current details on membership, see www.ascd.org/membership.

Library of Congress Cataloging-in-Publication Data

Names: Causton, Julie, author. | MacLeod, Kate, 1985- author.
Title: From behaving to belonging : the inclusive art of supporting
    students who challenge us / Julie Causton & Kate MacLeod.
Description: Alexandria, VA : ASCD, 2020. | Includes bibliographical
    references and index. | Summary: "This book helps teachers use love,
    acceptance, joy, and compassion to foster a sense of belonging among
    students who exhibit challenging behavior"—Provided by publisher.
Identifiers: LCCN 2020014013 (print) | LCCN 2020014014 (ebook) |
    ISBN 9781416629290 (paperback) | ISBN 9781416629313 (pdf)
Subjects: LCSH: Inclusive education. | Behavior modification. | Classroom
    environment. | Teacher-student relationships.
Classification: LCC LC1200 .C378 2020 (print) | LCC LC1200 (ebook) |
    DDC 371.9/046—dc23
LC record available at https://lccn.loc.gov/2020014013
LC ebook record available at https://lccn.loc.gov/2020014014

27 26 25 24 23 22 21 20   2 3 4 5 6 7 8 9 10 11 12

FROM BEHAVING TO BELONGING

A Note on Authorship

Authorship is traditionally listed in order of contribution to the piece. However, to honor the innovative, collaborative, and supportive nature of our professional relationship and friendship, we have listed authorship alphabetically.

Introduction

Love and Education: How Did We Get Here?

We decided to write this book together as a way to invite teachers to explore the practice of teaching and supporting students from a place of love. Every year, we conduct hundreds of workshops and presentations with administrators, educators, and parents around the country to help them develop loving and inclusive approaches to support diverse students. We wanted to share practices, stories, and tools from our experiences as people committed to teaching and leading schools from the heart.

We understand that it may seem radical for us to use words like *love*, *compassion*, and *heart* when we talk about behavior and discipline. However, we feel emboldened not only because the concept of love in education is not new but also because neuroscientists and biologists have begun to use this very same language in their research as they learn more about the significant impact love and compassion have on the human mind and body. Our brains are constantly forming and changing throughout our lives, and the human mind is particularly impressionable when we reach school age and adolescence. Educators, therefore, have the power to shape and change student brains at critical times in their lives. The compassionate words and actions we model and the heartfelt strategies we practice with our students can help shape who they are and, eventually, who they will become.

Many teachers and administrators, at their core, believe in teaching from the heart and leading with love. Yet they don't always know how teaching from the heart translates into effective supports and practices for working with students who exhibit challenging behavior. Over the years, we have drawn from incredible scholars and thinkers (such as Alfie Kohn, Bill Ayers, and bell hooks), expert practicing educators, wise and intuitive students, and formalized approaches (such as restorative practices, humanistic behavior supports, and social-emotional learning) to turn an educator's belief in love into actionable, practical, heartfelt practices that work to heal.

Why Do We Teach?

Because we have the incredible power and privilege to help shape student brains, it is critical that we ask ourselves the following questions: "What do we want for our students?" and "Who would we like to help them become?"

We have thought about this question long and hard, and we wanted to share our thinking with you as you begin to approach the question for yourself. We, Kate and Julie, teach because we believe we can

- Create inclusive and sacred environments where every one of our students can feel safe, valued, and loved.
- Encourage possibility, transformation, and creativity.
- Promote compassion and belonging in our students and communities.
- Build a society in which we celebrate the diversity of humanity.
- Help every human reach an even fuller version of their potential.

We also teach because we are hopeful and intent on living a life that aligns with our values. We teach because, although changing systems and communities can be daunting and seemingly impossible, we believe change begins with us.

And, above all else, we teach from a place of love.

Teaching Is Hard

Practicing love and compassion in education isn't always easy, and we are not pretending to sugarcoat the daily realities of a teacher. We know that educators are tasked with immeasurable work and incredibly challenging situations. You must be both generalists and specialists and be prepared to teach reading, writing, arithmetic, a variety of content areas, life skills, communication and collaboration skills, socioemotional skills, and remedial skills. You must meet national and state standards and help your students achieve on standardized assessments you may or may not agree with philosophically. You must be guides, inspirations, nurturers, comforters, critics, comedians, gurus, therapists, and advocates. You must show up every day, in every way, for each and every one of your students.

Educators must also come prepared to address students' fears, concerns, hearts, and minds. In recent years, educators have arrived at school, heartbroken themselves, to talk to their students about mass shootings at Parkland High School, a Pittsburgh synagogue, an Orlando nightclub, and a church in Charleston. Educators have shown up to discuss national movements and traumas connected to #BlackLivesMatter and #MeToo. And educators have shown up to listen to and support students dealing with community and personal issues—a bomb threat at the local high school, a young boy who lost his mother to breast cancer, or a student bullied for her transgender identity.

But let us not forget that educators also have the amazing opportunity to come to school and celebrate and experience joy with students—and to practice and teach kindness, love, and compassion. Educators such as you are there to give a student a hug after her first typed communication on her iPad and share a goofy dance with students at graduation. Educators such as you take a moment to help a student understand her anger and let her know they are there to support her no matter what. Educators such as you are there to shed happy tears when 10th graders present community action projects about ending homelessness. And you are there to show students how to spread kindness and gratitude to one another at the end of a hard day . . . or a wonderful day.

Throughout all this joy, pain, and love, if we are to use a heartfelt approach that draws on love, we must also face our triumphs and failures with kindness and compassion for our students and ourselves. We must reflect on our bravest moments and our most vulnerable ones. We must consider our language and our actions with our most challenging students. We must consider how to push back against systems or schools that do not align with our values or educational philosophies. And we must always ask, "How can we do this better tomorrow with more love and compassion?"

Throughout this book, we will ask you to practice the radical act of reclaiming your classroom as a place of love. We will ask you to consider new ways to approach your students with love and to teach them, with words and actions, the new types of learning and becoming that can occur when we bring love and education together.

Before reading on to the next section, we want you to take some time to answer the question of why you teach (see Figure 0.1). This will help ground and focus you before you dive into the perspectives, tools, and "how-tos" of our approach. Please be sure to reflect on all the amazing, artful, change-making work you take part in every day as a teacher. We encourage you to write or draw your response. Throughout this book, we will ask you to engage your learning in various ways with questions, reflections, and activities. We encourage you to dedicate a journal to use in connection with this book. Whenever you see this journal prompt icon, you can write, draw, and reflect in your journal.

Figure 0.1: Why Do I Teach?

Why This Book Matters Now

Even when excellent educators approach teaching from a place of love, we find that they can still struggle approaching students with challenging behavior from the same place. When we work with educators and administrators across the country, they almost always point to challenging behavior, outdated behavior management practices, and misguided schoolwide discipline policies that get in the way of effective, heartfelt teaching. Because challenging behavior is one of the most significant issues educators face, we know it is critical to rethink these outdated behavior management practices that do not align with educator values such as promoting inclusion and teaching with love.

Since the 1990s, school discipline approaches have largely been dominated by zero-tolerance policies. Originally developed as an approach to drug enforcement (Skiba & Rausch, 2006), zero-tolerance policies were adopted by schools as a way to uniformly mandate responses to student behavior, such as bullying, fighting, drugs, and disruption. However, such uniform responses are punitive and severe (e.g., suspension or expulsion) and are applied regardless of circumstances or context.

Educational and psychological research has shown again and again that zero-tolerance policies are not effective in creating safer schools. In fact, they often produce negative outcomes for students, such as a lack of opportunities to engage in school relationships, a distrust of adults, and a negative impact on self-worth and self-esteem (APA Zero Tolerance Task Force, 2008).

Pause now and consider your answers to our question "Why do I teach?" It is likely that the outcomes of zero-tolerance policies and practices do not align with your values. This is particularly true when we examine the following incredible personal and systemic challenges students are facing today in our schools:

- Reports of anxiety and depression among our school-aged students are at an all-time high (National Center for Education Statistics, 2019).
- One out of every five students report that they are bullied at school (National Center for Education Statistics, 2019), and the reasons most often cited by students include physical appearance, race and ethnicity, gender, disability, religion, and sexual orientation (National Center for Education Statistics, 2019).
- Students who are subjected to bias-based bullying are at a higher risk for negative emotional and physical health effects than students who report nonbias-based bullying (Rosenthal et al., 2015).
- Schools across the nation are suspending, excluding, and expelling students with disabilities, students of color, and LGBTQ students at a significantly higher rate than their nondisabled, white, and cisgendered peers (U.S. Department of Education, Office for Civil Rights, 2016).
- Our nation is politically divided with a significant focus on identity politics connected to race, religion, immigration status, gender, and sexual orientation.

These issues are overwhelming, and our current punitive behavior management and disciplinary practices only exacerbate them. In order to realize the values you've outlined in your response to "Why do I teach?"—and to reclaim your classroom as a sacred, heartfelt space—we must rethink and restory the way we understand and approach student behavior. Our students, now more than ever, need us to believe in them, shine a light on their strengths, and approach them with whole hearts and compassion every single day.

What's Different About Our Approach?

Our approach first requires you to shift away from a "behavior management" mindset that punishes or rewards students for "good" or "compliant" behavior. We then ask you to adopt new heartfelt approaches that foster a sense of belonging and aim to support all students, even the *most* challenging ones, with kindness, creativity, compassion, and love.

When we support a student using a heartfelt approach, we

- Focus on the student's strengths, gifts, and talents.
- Brainstorm and enact strategies that illuminate and create deeper connections between teacher and student.
- Implement strategies that illuminate and create deeper connections between a student and their peers.
- Purposefully plan to ignite the student's creativity and sense of self-worth.
- Problem solve daily to meet the social, emotional, and academic needs of the learner.

Rather than use outdated behavioral management practices such as rewards and punishments, our approach

- Helps you reconnect to your values and beliefs about students and teaching.
- Helps you identify barriers to student success in the cultural, social, and environmental landscape.
- Provides questions for rethinking challenging student behavior and how we support our students.
- Is steeped in the extreme self-care of the educator first.

When we use an approach that focuses on belonging, we are teaching and leading from a place of love. This book represents a paradigm shift from a punitive mindset to a strengths-based, loving approach and represents a radical act toward creating more inclusive and caring schools.

Who We Are

We, Kate and Julie, are here to guide you as you explore what leading with your heart to support students with challenging behavior means for you. For the past several decades, we have worked as teachers, researchers, and consultants to support administrators, educators, students, and parents through the art of creating caring, creative, and inclusive schools for all learners. We are in schools across the country working alongside teachers who are supporting students with some of the most challenging behaviors.

Does This Book Fit with Existing Approaches?

This book is an excellent complement to the strategies and ideas involved in Positive Behavioral Interventions and Supports (PBIS) and Restorative Practices in Schools (RP). It is not a replacement of these ideas but instead a deeper complement and personal guide to help teachers embrace all types of behavioral supports that focus on belonging, acceptance, relationships, and building an inclusive school culture.

PBIS consists of clearly defining and teaching behavioral expectations and rewarding positive behavior. It also focuses on targeted interventions consistent with expectations. For students with more intense behavioral support needs, it utilizes a wrap-around approach guided by a functional behavioral assessment. Our approach works hand in glove with these ideas, but it also provides a deeper framework of emotional supports to educators as they do this work.

RP, like our approach, focuses on shifting from the use of punitive strategies to handle student behavior, using alternative methods grounded in building positive relationships between teachers and students, and helping students problem solve conflicts and emotions. Schools using RP can implement specific methods, such as informal problem-solving conversations, circles, and mediation to help students reflect on their behaviors, take responsibility for what happened, and work collaboratively to determine a plan to address any harm done to the student, peers, teachers, or community. Emergent research regarding the effectiveness of restorative practices shows that the use of RP can reduce disciplinary issues and improve the academic and social culture of a school community.

Our approach parallels the RP mindset shift from punitive to positive and provides expanded problem-solving methods and conversations you can have with your students and your colleagues. When used alongside RP, our approach and practices will help you deepen your ability to build positive and authentic relationships with your students.

How to Use This Book

As you make your way through each section of this book, we will provide you with heartfelt strategies, variations, and examples you can try with both individual students and entire classrooms. We believe the ideas in this book are powerful tools for change, and we encourage you to spend time reading, analyzing, and practicing them. We have provided stories from teachers, students, and families we've worked with in each chapter (though we have changed some names and details). Our deepest thanks go out to all those who provided their voices and support for this work and this book. The stories are critical because we believe the experiences of these individuals are what best bring our approach and its dramatic results to life.

Chapter Contents

Chapter 1: Rethinking Students Who Challenge Us. This foundational chapter is about the active work teachers must engage in to rethink our students' challenging behavior using a heartfelt, strengths-based approach. We explore the ways in which schooling systems, traditional disability labels, and deficit-based thinking can stifle educators' natural inclination to support students in creative and loving ways. We then describe a new approach to view difference and diversity as natural and positive. We provide practices to help reset thinking and lead to a change in student support.

Chapter 2: Focusing on Educators' Mental Health: Developing Love and Self-Care. When our cup is full, it is easier to share with others. We want educators who have full cups. Students deserve educators who are rested and in the right emotional place to support them with love and kindness. That requires a good deal of reflective self-care. Dealing with challenging behavior can feel very personal and emotionally taxing. We provide strategies and supports for you to reflect on each day and to process and heal the challenging emotions that come from this difficult work.

Chapter 3: Belonging: Putting Your Love on Display. In this chapter, we discuss the structures and practices in traditional schooling that can impede a sense of belonging for many of our students. These include pullout programs for students with disabilities and English language learners, separate classrooms for students with behavior problems, and ability grouping. We contrast these with inclusive structures and practices that foster a sense of belonging and connections to peers and teachers. These structures and practices help educators cultivate relationships, facilitate collaboration, encourage friendships, and celebrate what is unique about each learner.

Chapter 4: Creating a Culture of Inclusion. In this chapter, we ask you to abandon the myth of the so-called typical learner and embrace diversity in new ways in the classroom. We discuss that, as educators, what we do and present in our classrooms (i.e., instruction, curriculum, language, materials, community building) has a significant effect on student behavior. We discuss class and school-wide practices that educators can draw on to decrease challenging behavior, create an inclusive culture, and respect who students are and the value they bring to the school community.

Chapter 5: Teaching Gratitude, Kindness, and Compassion. Here, we focus on how you can teach students important social and emotional skills such as kindness, compassion, gratitude, and trust. We provide strategies, ideas, and resources you can use daily in your classrooms or throughout the entire school. We address what research says about these practices and how they connect deeply to our goal of building kinder, compassionate, and more inclusive communities.

Chapter 6: Exploring Acceptance, Belonging, and Community: Heartfelt Problem Solving. In this chapter, we focus on shifting from a mindset of fixing or disciplining student behavior to collaborative problem solving *with* the student. We ask educators to reflect on their responses to student behavior and invest in building relationships—instead of barriers—with students. We discuss practices that support educators to do this work, including giving students and families ownership over the process, encouraging peers to work together to develop new ideas and mediate existing problems (which aligns well with RP), and leading colleagues to help create success plans for students.

Chapter 7: Dealing with Crisis Artfully. The goal of this book is to help students be seen, heard, and supported so they do not end up in emotional crisis. However, even with thoughtful planning, creative and engaging lessons, and a cohesive community, some students will still struggle with behavior. The most important thing educators can do is accept that fact and respond in a compassionate, calm, and loving way. When a student struggles and is yelling, hitting, or kicking, we explain that safety is the primary concern. We then ask educators to reflect on how they would want someone to react to an extremely difficult situation or an emotional meltdown. This chapter deals with the practices that come in handy during a crisis.

Chapter 8: Proclaiming and Maintaining Loving Spaces. The book concludes with inspiration for committing to the work and practices you can use to increase your happiness, improve your health, and build a more connected community of educators. We know that educators who are happier and more connected to a support network are better able to support students. We therefore conclude with two "educator proclamations" for creating and sustaining radical and loving classrooms.

Helpful Tools for Using This Book

Throughout the book, we encourage you to write, highlight, and draw on these pages to help clarify your thinking and engage in the many self-assessment and reflection sections we've included. You will also find reproducibles, such as the following:

- Our strengths-based approach protocol for supporting students.
- Our collaborative heartfelt problem-solving process.
- Examples of heartfelt problem-solving processes and success plans.
- Teacher proclamations for committing to loving, caring classrooms.

Take Your Time

We hope that by the end of the book, our approach and the tools we've provided will help you feel empowered and encouraged to develop deeper relationships with students, promote desired student behavior, and improve an inclusive classroom community and culture for all. Take your time and feel free to jump around to sections you need right away. This book's primary goal is to support you with love and compassion—because you are a teacher and a superhero.

Tiny To-Do List

In each chapter, we share a Tiny To-Do List to help you focus on ways to implement big ideas and practices from each chapter. Your first Tiny To-Do list is as follows:

❐ Dedicate a journal you can use in connection with this book.

❐ Reflect on and write your reflections for "Why do I teach?"

❐ Reflect on and write about what you would like to get out of reading this book.

❐ Do something kind for yourself this week, such as reading a book, taking a walk, meeting a friend, or meditating.

Rethinking Students Who Challenge Us

If we are to reclaim our classrooms as inclusive and loving spaces where all students are valued and celebrated, we must actively work on rethinking our students' challenging behavior using a strengths-based, holistic, and loving approach. In this chapter, we aim to shift from a traditional deficit-based way of understanding kids with challenging behavior and instead describe new ways of thinking about student differences, including approaching behaviors as natural and expected means of communication. We then help you focus on the strengths, gifts, and talents of each student and provide specific ways of being and practices to help you reset and reinvigorate your thinking about students with challenging behavior. This approach helps us boost and lean into our natural inclination to support students in creative and loving ways.

Value Student Differences

The richness of our classrooms, schools, and communities is derived from difference. In a classroom community that operates from a place of love, we've watched it take only a few moments for students to notice, learn about, and embrace one another's differences. Often, this process of understanding and valuing difference uses a similar pattern with groups of students:

- Students noticing something *different* about a peer.
- Students becoming *curious* about that difference.
- Students learning what that difference means for how to *engage and connect* with the peer.
- Students *embracing* the difference and the peer.

We see students engage in this loving work every day. In 2017, a video from BBC News (2017) began circulating the internet and perfectly documented this natural peer process of embracing differences. A group of students greet their classmate Anu as she walks to the playground for the first time with her new prosthetic leg. Her peers bend down to take a look at her new neon pink titanium leg. They ask questions such as, "Did it hurt?" and "Did you pick the color?" They embrace her in hugs. The young girl then shows them how she can run with her new leg. Then her peers begin to run beside her and behind her, matching her pace. Soon, she is leading the way. This brief video ends with the young girl and a peer walking hand in hand.

We can learn so much from our students about how quickly and readily they embrace and celebrate differences (in the case above, in 42 seconds). But first, we must provide students with the opportunity to interact with and embrace one another's differences so they can lean into their strengths and talents and learn from and grow with one another. Students' readiness to embrace differences can often be stifled by school cultures and structures that focus on the concept of normalcy; consequently, schools often sort and separate students with differences before the peer community even has a chance to love and embrace them. The first step is breaking down the myth of normal.

No Student Is Bad

It is this mythical concept of normal that can too often perpetuate barriers for our students' success. It can impede our ability to value student diversity and instead label it as different, challenging, or deficient. Perhaps the most pressing issue with labeling a student as challenging or deficient is that none of these labels are ever true. Isn't that refreshing? Our students are not challenging, bad, or naughty. Instead, student actions and behaviors, influenced by a contextual stew of socioemotional, academic, environmental, and disability-specific factors, *present* as challenging or disruptive.

In other words, we must remember that kids are not bad. All kids want to be loved and understood. All challenging behavior is merely evidence of kids asking us for that love and understanding in a way they know how. The more significant the presentation of behavior, the more we need to use love, support, and understanding in order to address the student's needs.

All Students Want Love and Understanding

All students want love and understanding, so it is critical to rethink deficit-based thinking about students and student behavior. We're sure you have, at some point, said or heard a teacher say something like, "He's an attention seeker. He only acts out because he knows it will get him attention from the teacher or his peers." This is a very common way to describe and explain students and their behavior. Ultimately, though, this way of thinking is fundamentally flawed. Consider the following examples:

> **Deficit-based thinking:** We assume only kids with challenging behavior seek attention from adults and peers.

> **Truth:** *All* kids seek attention. Attention is proof that we are loved and understood, which is a fundamental need for all humans.

> **Deficit-based thinking:** We assume that kids only display the challenging behavior because it gets them something (i.e., attention).

> **Truth:** All students would display the expected behavior if they knew how to get attention in appropriate and expected ways. The student exhibiting the challenging behavior simply doesn't have the skills, tools, or knowledge about how to display the appropriate behavior yet.

Let's look at another common phrase we sometimes say or hear about students with challenging behavior in teachers' lounges and meetings: "She's manipulative. She asks me questions that have nothing to do with the lesson, argues with me, and tells me all about what other kids are doing wrong. She often says, 'The other kids don't like the way I talk about them, so they avoid me.' And I know she does all this just to avoid work!"

Again, we understand the student's behavior is working in her favor! But here, too, this deficit-based thinking about a student and her behavior is fundamentally flawed. Let's consider another set of beliefs around student behavior:

Deficit-based thinking: We assume that kids who display challenging behavior have planned the behaviors out using skillful forethought, impulse control, planning, and organization.

Truth: Most of us behave in ways to get our needs met. That does not make us manipulative. Most students with challenging behavior don't have the very skills (i.e., impulse control, planning, and organization) needed to manipulate an outcome. In fact, if the kid had those skills, she would most likely be able to attend to the tasks at hand (e.g., focusing on the lesson and building positive relationships with peers) and avoid getting in trouble and isolating herself from peers.

Rethinking the deficit-based approach to working with students that attempts to incorrectly identify student behavior as normal or abnormal, good or bad, or malicious or innocent is the first step in reclaiming our classrooms as places of love. We must commit to the understanding that all kids want to behave because they all want love, understanding, and success. For kids with challenging behavior, we must remember that they want to attend to the math task like you've asked. They want to engage with peers in appropriate ways that lead to strong peer connections and friendships. They want to have positive relationships with adults, including you. But for kids with challenging behavior, they might not have the specific skills, prior knowledge, or opportunities to succeed in the ways in which schools expect them to succeed and behave.

Kids Do Well if They Can

Ross Greene, a scholar who writes and speaks with great expertise about how to implement better, more effective ways to work with kids with challenging behavior, explains in his important school-based text *Lost at School* (2008) that we must shift our thinking from "Kids do well if they want to" to "Kids do well if they can" (p. 10). This paradigm shift is powerful because it helps us reimagine our students using a strengths-based and compassionate perspective.

When we realize that all students want to do well, it helps us approach students in new ways. Even when students are demonstrating that they don't care or don't want to try, we must look past the actual behaviors and language to the meaning behind it. Students might act as if they don't care because they are fearful they won't be successful. Students might say they hate us because they are scared we will be disappointed in them. Supporting a student who is scared or anxious is much different than looking at the behavior as defiance or manipulation. We not only need to rethink student motivations; we also need to reexamine our larger structures that are based on the myth of normalcy.

Normalcy Is a Myth

In schools across the country, the concept of "normal" often marginalizes students based on issues of differences, such as perceived ability, behavior, race, and language. We often do it with the best of intentions, but it still happens. The student with dyslexia who doesn't read as well or as quickly as her peers is often educated in a segregated reading room down the hall. The student who is more verbal than others is told again and again to be quiet. The African American boy who displays challenging behavior in a predominately white school can be quickly disciplined, or even wrongly labeled with an emotional disturbance. Though there are many issues to grapple with in these examples, ultimately, they represent the damage deficit-based thinking can inflict on student structures such as placement, labeling, rules, policies, regulations, and ideas about what students can be.

The more equitable, effective, and loving way to work with kids with diverse backgrounds, abilities, and needs—including behavioral needs—builds on the peer process of diversity acceptance we shared earlier. First, we acknowledge that difference is the norm. This means that normal behavior, normal academic achievement, normal communication styles, and normal social skills—frankly, whatever you are attempting to normalize!—are myths. You and your students are thankfully too diverse and amazing to behave, move, think, communicate, and interact in the same standardized ways.

It is often easy for us to value diversity, but when it comes to students with challenging behavior, it is common for us to quickly jump to conclusions and beliefs about the student. Instead of these knee-jerk reactions when we are faced with behaviors that challenge us, we must pause and take the time to acknowledge and value the individual differences that have carried the student to this particular point in her life, education, and, of course, the specific challenging behaviors.

Embracing diversity means we must also abandon the idea that normal behavior is the only valuable behavior. This idea can be very hard because we know classroom disruptions happen due to challenging behavior, and we'd rather those disruptions didn't happen at all. But if we take a moment to reimagine our well-behaved students and expand our thinking to include all our students, even if they have challenging behaviors, we then begin to *expect* that all our students will behave differently and will need to learn different skills.

If students are only valued when they are quiet and compliant learners, never question our authority, and do what they're told, we run the significant risk of devaluing and underestimating too many of our students. Instead, when we seek to understand the whole student, we can begin to celebrate how they show up every day, even *without* all the skills it might take to succeed the way they'd like to (or in the ways we'd like them to). Only then can we begin to consciously create a classroom environment that values and addresses not only the needs of our diverse students but also the individuality they each bring to our world. Only then can we truly begin to understand our students as valuable—not despite the individual ways they move, think, play, and communicate but because of those differences.

Star the Strengths

Often, our kids with challenging behavior can spend the majority of their days being told what they're doing wrong and how to do it—whatever it is—the "right" way. Sit still. Be quiet. Do your work. Walk in a straight line. Write neatly. Speak clearly. Raise your hand. It can be exhausting for educators and students. When we hyperfocus on fixing the behaviors and require kids to achieve that mythical norm, we often miss out on opportunities to give them a chance to nurture talents and skills. Let's push against the traditional school mode of obedience and lean into radical love in the classroom. We begin by starring students' strengths.

Carve out time and space to help students develop and build upon what they are interested in and good at. Starring the strengths helps you to approach students from a place of love and respect, and it helps you build their confidence so they feel, perhaps even for the first time, successful and confident at school. For example, take the way 10th grade teacher, Patrice Smith, approached a student named Song and starred her strengths to help address challenging behavior and simultaneously improve her feelings of success and belonging.

Song was often in the principal's office for "defiant and loud class disruptions," particularly during her English class with her ELA teacher, Tom. Tom was at his wits' end because, as he said, "Song is such a bright student, a good student, but she just can't keep it together in ELA. And with her outbursts, I just can't have her constantly disrupting the class. I don't know what to do." Song's geometry teacher, Kim, knew Song to be an excellent student with minimal to no disruptions in class. Kim suggested that she and Tom brainstorm about Song's strengths and talents together. They discovered that Song

- Is a strong student who loves math and problem solving.
- Has two younger siblings and works very well with younger students.
- Loves comic books.
- Is interested in her Asian American heritage.
- Is musical.
- Is a kinesthetic learner and likes to move about when working.
- Is a leader among her peers.

Maybe you're thinking that you're at the beginning of the school year and you couldn't possibly know all the relevant information about a student yet, not to mention a list of their talents and strengths. We recommend engaging students in this work by asking them to think through their strengths and talents during class meetings or morning circles, or even by handing out a survey or multiple intelligence quiz in class. These practices can help students identify and star their own strengths, talents, and interests so they know how best they can learn, interact, and grow.

Once you do this with your entire class, you can create a positive student profile that helps you understand particular students with challenging behavior from a restoried, strengths-based perspective. By using Figure 1.1, we recommend writing this positive student profile with the student to make sure everything is accurate and true and that they feel a part of the process. Sometimes, this might require support from family, siblings, and friends. Keep in mind that the information in the profile should be used to create new ways and opportunities for the student to build on their strengths and interests and, ultimately, to shine in your classroom.

Figure 1.1: Song's Positive Student Profile

STRENGTHS, TALENTS, AND INTERESTS

- Is a strong student who loves math and solving problems
- Is bilingual
- Has two younger siblings and works very well with younger students
- Loves comic books
- Loves K-Pop
- Is interested in her Asian American heritage
- Is a leader among her peers

MULTIPLE INTELLIGENCES

- Has logical-mathematical intelligence
- Has musical intelligence
- Is a kinesthetic learner and likes to move when working

ACADEMIC SUBJECT INFORMATION

- Is very strong in math and science
- Excels in art and music class
- Loves science and maintains a 99% average
- Loves lab assignments, especially when she is the lab leader
- Reads English independently at two grade levels below her peers
- Has a reading comprehension level one grade level above her peers with access to audio, text, and read-alouds

SOCIAL INFORMATION

- Has some close friends
- Still has learning strategies for dealing with conflict

FAMILY INFORMATION

- Lives with her parents, grandmother, and three elementary-aged younger siblings
- Moved from South Korea when she was in elementary school

SPECIAL EDUCATION SERVICES OR ACCOMMODATIONS (IF APPLICABLE)

- Has been labeled with a specific learning disability in reading
- Has access to accommodations for audio text, text-to-speech prompts, tests, and read alouds
- Receives consultant support from special education teacher regarding reading supports

(continues)

Figure 1.1: Song's Positive Student Profile *(continued)*

STRATEGIES THAT WORK

- Allowed to take frequent breaks (up to three per class)
- Responds to asking her what she needs when she seems upset
- Reacts well to calm, loving responses to her behavior
- Allowed to listen to music
- Has access to audiobooks and texts
- Has access to partnered reading
- Needs help resetting behavior after an outburst

Restory the Challenging Behavior

Next, you'll want to practice restorying the student's challenging behavior. To begin this work, we ask you to join us in a short exercise. Use Figure 1.2 to look over some of the most challenging behaviors educators consistently highlight. However, instead of asking whether you have seen your students display these challenging behaviors in your own classroom, we'd instead like you to circle any of the behaviors you *yourself* have engaged in over the years—as a student, an employee, a family member, a friend, or a community member.

If you're anything like us, you might have circled several of these challenging behaviors. This also means you are perfectly human. The fact that you've engaged in some challenging behavior in your life doesn't mean you are not a valued student, employee, partner, parent, or friend. It simply means you were communicating something at the time. Perhaps, at that time, you didn't have all the necessary skills and tools to understand your behaviors or manage them to the best of your ability.

Figure 1.2: Identifying Challenging Behavior

• Yelling	• Challenging authority
• Fighting	• Talking back
• Throwing items	• Swearing
• Avoiding work	• Talking out of turn
• Leaving or storming out of the room	• Talking to your neighbor when the expectation is that you should be listening to the speaker
• Shutting down or closing off	

Talking to the person next to you during a faculty meeting might have communicated that the principal had gone on too long about the new literacy program and you needed a chance to actively engage with another person rather than passively absorb. Yelling at a spouse might communicate that you are angry or not OK and need new and improved skills to help communicate anger or pain more effectively.

Now, turn this same understanding toward student behavior. Throwing something across the room might communicate she is not OK and needs support and new skills to better communicate her anger, confusion, or pain. Likewise, running out of the room and turning desks over on the way out after an altercation with a peer might communicate that the student is angry and embarrassed. Perhaps her peers didn't know or understand that she needed a note-taking accommodation during work time. Perhaps she wanted to socialize but doesn't have all the skills required to do so yet.

Remember, kids do well if they can. All kids want to do well because they want love, belonging, and understanding. It is up to us to restory our students' challenging behavior in order to help them succeed, feel loved, and feel understood. Certainly, it's what we'd want someone to do for us.

To set you up for success with the practice of restorying challenging behavior, we've provided a few simple questions we'd like you to follow. We will continue to use Song as an example for the process.

What is the challenging behavior? (Be as specific as possible.) Song is disruptive (e.g., she interrupts, curses, or refuses to participate) during reading activities in English class. This often results in her leaving class to visit the principal's office or cool down.

What do we know about the student that might inform the challenging behavior? Song has a specific learning disability in reading. She was identified as an English language learner when she arrived from South Korea three years ago. She excels in math but utilizes text-to-speech applications to help her work through word problems and new math vocabulary.

How can we restory this behavior as communication?

- Song doesn't feel confident in her reading skills.
- Song doesn't yet know how to ask for or doesn't have the opportunity to access her accommodations such as text-to-speech applications or audio text during her English class.

- Song doesn't feel like she can succeed in English class.
- Song feels like she doesn't belong in English class.

You can see that when we restoried Song's behavior as communication, we didn't include stories like "Song is unmotivated in English" or "Song is manipulative and relies on behavior to get out of English work and class." Instead, we restoried her behavior as communication from a place where she is only seeking success, connection, and belonging. Use Figure 1.3 to see how you can begin restorying your students' experiences.

Figure 1.3: Using Restorying Questions

1. What is the challenging behavior? (Be as specific as possible.)
2. What do we know about the student that might inform the challenging behavior?
3. How can we restory this behavior as communication?

Learn from Student Behavior

A critical and integrated step is to move from restorying the behavior to learning from the behavior. Once you begin to practice from the mindset that behavior is communication, you must then deeply listen, observe, ask, and learn about the behaviors—and the student as a whole person. By using these practices, you can begin to pinpoint the communicative intent in collaboration with the student and respond by providing loving and creative supports and tools. This might mean we ask the student a direct question about their behavior such as, "Song, it must mean something when you put your head down on your desk after I've asked everyone to independently read. Can you tell me what it means for you?"

Another strategy is to watch and make hypotheses about the communicative purpose of the behavior. This is similar to what we did when we were restorying the behavior. When creating hypotheses, always consider the most positive potential purpose for behavior that remains consistent with the facts. For example, consider a student's need for joy, choice, control, sense of belonging, positive relationships, interdependence, independence, expressions of frustration, and access to communication as potential purposes of behavior.

Consider also that the challenging behavior is displayed because the student, perhaps due to disability, language, culture, trauma, or any number of inter-connected and complex factors, does not have the skills or tools with which to communicate, process, or regulate their emotions or behavior in a way that schools or educators deem appropriate. Remember that kids do well if they can, and we must always assume that students do *not* have a malicious or manipulative intent. We must believe they are simply trying to have their needs met and, in some cases, merely survive. If colleagues disagree with you, you can point them to empirical evidence that shows behavior is linked to a mismatch between student needs and classroom expectations, activity, schedule, or environment (Epstein, Atkins, Cullinan, Kutash, & Weaver, 2008). Alternatively, you can say that you choose to believe this because you are reclaiming your classroom as a place of love and therefore must look for the positive intent in your students.

Expand Your Perspective and Give It Time

If we are to commit to supporting students from a place of love, we must widen our lens of understanding and address the greater context of factors affecting the student. We must dive deep into learning about students' preferences, talents, and interests; their family context; the way they interact with the curriculum; our instruction and teaching style; and the social landscape of our classroom, school community, and larger community. When challenging behavior occurs, in order to consider the most loving response, we must try to understand how the behavior is connected to all these factors.

Not only is this hard work, it also takes time. We must practice patience because knowing about students and providing supports doesn't mean the behaviors will stop right away. Just as it takes practice to learn new math and reading skills, it also takes students time to learn new skills to express their emotions, needs, and wants.

Apply the Golden Rule

 The golden rule for supporting students with challenging behavior in schools is to support them just as you would want to be supported. Remember the exercise we did earlier in the chapter where we asked you to circle some of the challenging behaviors you have displayed?

Now we're going to ask you the follow-up question: "What was it I needed in that moment?" Go ahead and get out your journal to respond.

Did you need a hug? The benefit of the doubt? A friend to listen to you? A chance to escape the faculty meeting? Someone to help you outline the difficult task ahead of you? A nap? A snack? Whatever it was you answered, we imagine that your responses did not align with what so often is provided to students in schools with challenging behavior—angry words and body language, physical redirection, limited recess, a visit to the principal, a punitive call home, lunch or afterschool detention, a suspension. The issue is, we know these don't often work. Paula Kluth (2010) even argues that a "punitive approach almost always serves to distance the teacher from the student and certainly fails to strengthen their relationship. It is ironic, but true, that the more a teacher may try to control a situation [or behavior], the more out of control that situation may become" (p. 22). Instead, as educators, we must practice the Golden Rule with our students if we are to reclaim our classrooms as places of love.

Be Conscious of Your Language

As poet Gregory Orr says, "Words build worlds," so we must be incredibly conscious of the words we use about and with our students.

Using Writing

Consider the words written about students who have challenging behavior. We might see a long list of deficits, disorders, and problems written in indelible ink in a student's IEP. Each sentence represents a problem or situation that gets recorded in that student's permanent record. We would like you to rethink that practice and instead record all the student's gifts, strengths, and positive attributes. When we write about students in these ways, we can actually restory a student's future.

Using Personal Communication

We like to stick to the following three guidelines when communicating, regardless of the age of the person with whom we are connecting.

1. **Use positive and loving language.** Using positive language with students helps frame the way they will think about themselves, respond to us, and interact with one another. If we use negative deficit-based language with

students, they internalize it and respond accordingly with self-doubt, a negative self-image, and deficit-based language with us and peers.

2. **Be honest, specific, and direct.** Students in our care deserve our respect and love, and that means we must be honest, specific, and direct with them. Phrases like "Great job" and "Try harder" are vague and don't mean anything to students or to us. If we want students to understand that telling a peer they're a "retard" isn't OK in a classroom grounded in love and respect, we must shift our response from "We don't use that word, Peter" to "Our class expectation is that everyone is treated with love and respect in here." It is also important to know that the conversation doesn't end there. Having a private conversation with Peter later or even scheduling a class meeting to revisit the type of language and respect expected in class is an important follow-up step.

3. **Use inclusive language.** This may seem like a no brainer, but it is so important to use inclusive language in all its forms. Spend the time to learn the correct pronunciation of all your students' names and their preferred pronouns. Always use age-appropriate language with students and speak directly to them—not to teaching assistants, paraprofessionals, or other educators. Use a student's native language in everyday conversation and make sure your curriculum, whenever possible, represents the cultures, genders, and racial makeup of your class. Make sure to avoid isolating phrases such as "Tell your mom and dad" because so many of our students have unique family constellations, whether it is two moms or dads, grandparents, a single parent, or a legal guardian.

You likely have other guidelines for communication and language you use to help focus on empowering your students, building their confidence, and creating an environment of belonging. We encourage you to continue building that practice and sharing with your students, colleagues, and families.

Learn to Love

Sometimes we need to dig deep to star student's strengths and restory their challenging behavior. Even if you *want* to love all your students, it might take more time and effort to accomplish that goal. But if you are to reclaim your classroom as a place of love, we ask you to change your thinking about what it means to love a student. Attempt to create a love that is resilient and unconditional. A love that doesn't depend on the student's behaviors or daily moods. If you can approach all students with this type of unconditional love, you can more readily embrace their challenging behaviors with humor, curiosity, and empathy. You can clean up the mess and give a hug. You can know it's OK for you to be disappointed sometimes— or even often. You can embrace the knowledge that learning new skills takes time and patience—both for you and them.

There is much about teaching that can make us feel like giving up, but when you love your students, it is easier to find strength. In fact, in bell hooks's powerful book *all about love* (2000), she writes, "Knowing love or the hope of knowing love is the anchor that keeps us from falling into [that] sea of despair."

We believe that all endeavors to teach your students to be creative, compassionate, and thoughtful critical thinkers will be in vain if you cannot show up for them with love and give them the hope that goes along with being loved. This is particularly important to recognize when they are communicating to you through challenging behavior that they need new skills, tools, relationships, and love. We know that education is much more intimate than is often discussed. Every day, we work to develop intellectual and emotional connections with our students and engage them in discussions and problem solving that will help nurture their love of self and community.

We must not manage our classrooms. We must learn to love our students.

Recognize the Difference We Make Six Hours a Day

When we open ourselves to working with and loving our students, we also open ourselves to heartbreak regarding all they are going through. Many of our students have experienced more trauma and heartache than we have. When working in schools, it is common to experience personal heartbreak because we feel helpless to deal with forces outside school that negatively affect our students' mental, physical, and emotional health, such as homelessness, addiction, unmet mental health needs, abuse, incarceration of family members, and so much more.

As an open-hearted and loving educator, these feelings of heartbreak and hopelessness are normal and natural. Worry and loss of sleep over our students is part of being a compassionate human being. Compassion fatigue is what we label an extreme state of tension caused by helping. It evidences a focus on the suffering of those in need to the degree that it can be felt as a secondary trauma.

In the research about strategies used in effective trauma-informed schools, educators are encouraged to practice preventative measures through self-care (we will address this topic in greater detail in Chapter 2) and increased awareness and identification of secondary trauma symptoms, such as feeling overwhelmed, hopelessness, fatigue, engaging in self-destructive coping strategies, low job morale, and withdrawing from relationships with colleagues or family.

Self-care and awareness are important strategies to prevent or deal with secondary trauma, as is connecting with your colleagues and friends. Tracy, a teacher we know who works in a middle school with a high rate of students dealing with trauma, started a Teachers Supporting Teachers group at his school. Every Monday after the bell rings, the group gets together to check in about how they are doing, share self-care strategies, and simply connect and recharge with one another. Tracy said that for something that wasn't all that difficult to organize or execute, it has done miraculous things for his morale and well-being. Beyond caring for yourself and connecting with others, it is also important to ground yourself in all you *do* have control over when it comes to your students.

We have over six hours a day to make a difference in the lives of our students. We have six hours per day to fill a student up with love and hope. We have 360 minutes a day or 21,600 seconds per day to change their lives in ways beyond our imagination. It is unknowable what can be accomplished for a student in that amount of time. The hugs, the high fives, the handshakes, the wiping of tears, the positive messages of "You can do this" and "You are deserving of love and belonging" all make a significant difference. You may be one of many people in a kid's life who provides them with a foundation of love and kindness, or you may be the only one. If we remember that our main goal is to build, support, love, and connect, then our teaching, our students, and our relationships in schools can flourish.

Rock Your Support of Students

In a recent presentation with a large group of educators, we brought large landscaping rocks, each the size of a person's hand, and set them in the middle of each table. We explained the following Rock Rules:

1. Put a rock in your dominant hand.
2. Do not set the rock down.

3. Hold the rock the entire time.

4. Do not mention your rock.

5. Bring your rock with you everywhere.

Each table group had someone designated to be sure that their tablemates followed the rules. Then, all the participants had to continue to participate in the rest of the conference. Some of the activities involved groups working together to build a tower with paper and tape, whereas other activities included individual tasks such as taking notes. If a participant did not follow one of the Rock Rules, they were to come to the front of the large room and write their name on the "Warning Wall." After the morning activities and lunch had concluded, we told the group it was OK to set down their rocks and discuss the experience.

We began by talking about what the rocks represented, explaining that students all carry rocks. We asked this group of educators to consider the rocks their students carry. They responded by saying that these were things that weigh students down and shared examples such as trauma, anxiety, anger, depression, stress, pregnancy, body image, isolation, homelessness, addiction issues, disability labels, poverty, sexual identity, gender identity, and mental health issues. To say the least, they came up with a lot of different kinds and sizes for the rocks.

We then discussed what it was like for them to have carried rocks all morning. The educators described being very distracted by the rocks. It was stressful attempting to keep the rocks secret. The rocks also significantly influenced their ability to stay focused and connected to the learning.

"The rock impeded my ability to do *anything* it seemed," one educator said.

Another educator said, "I am quite struck by how difficult this was, especially because I knew that, at any time, I could set down my rock if I had to." He paused and then noted, "My students don't have that luxury."

What We Can't Do with Students' Rocks

We can't hold students' rocks for them, regardless of how much we want to take away the pain of struggle. If we attempt to hold all our students' challenges and concerns, two things happen. First, they do not learn how to carry and manage those issues, and second, we cannot function well when we are carrying the load of our students' rocks.

We can't pity students for their rocks. Pity is not useful for students. When we pity our students, we diminish their lived experiences and the resilience it can bring. Likewise, we can't spend our time blaming others for the rocks. Blame is not useful in schools. It is not useful to blame parents, caregivers, or situations. Instead, we can invest every breath in making our classroom experiences more accessible and compassionate for students.

We can't group students by rocks. It is commonplace in schools to place students with the biggest rocks in the same room. However, this practice decreases the natural diversity and all the richness that comes from learning with and from people who are different from us, as well as those who may have fewer rocks to carry. Additionally, this homogenous grouping practice creates a stigma. Students quickly learn that their classroom is indeed a place for students who struggle with the biggest rocks. Lastly, students learn best from peers who can be models. For example, perhaps a student's rock is about learning to build positive social relationships. This student will best learn this skill when she is surrounded by others who interact and socialize well.

What We Can Do with Students' Rocks

We can make space for their rocks and acknowledge and witness them. Recently, when we were presenting and doing the rock activity with a group of educators, a teacher who was clearly frustrated came up to us during the presentation and said, "I just can't NOT talk about this rock! The direction of secrecy is killing me. I can't listen to what you are saying or do anything else, really. Please, can we talk about them now?"

When we keep quiet about the rocks, we increase the challenge the rock presents for the student who carries it. Instead, we must create safe and open spaces where students are free to share their struggles.

We would love to be able to teach students that they can set their rocks down, but that option is often not possible. Instead, we can teach students that their rocks do not have to sink them or weigh them down. We can teach them that once we acknowledge the rock, we can then work together to create supports to make the challenge of carrying it more manageable. For example, if a student is currently homeless and living in a shelter, we can be sure to discuss it with her. Yes, it is a huge rock; it's a challenge she has no control over that can cause feelings of helplessness and hopelessness. But we are there to support her, provide extended deadlines for work, offer lunches and snacks, make her laugh, ditch the homework, and expect great things from her.

We can also help students build with their rocks. We can help them arrange their rocks into giant structures called *inuksuk*. An inuksuk is an Inuit practice of rock building where rocks are stacked into human form and placed in spaces where it is hard to travel. When you come across an inuksuk, it means "Someone has come before you." In other words, for some students, we can help them know that they are not alone, that others have traversed this path before, and that they have survived.

We can also examine our own rocks. Take some time and answer the question "What rocks do you carry?" Most of us carry many challenges, even if we have not taken those rocks out to look at in a while. How are you supporting yourself? Are you able to carry your own load of rocks, or do you need other kinds of support?

Finally, we can celebrate rocks. Lucy, a student we know, turned her rock of Obsessive-Compulsive Disorder (OCD) into several beautiful works of art. Painting her rock onto a canvas opened her up to a deeper understanding of her experiences and challenges. Each brush stroke helped her see how OCD affects her life. She was able to explore the weight of her OCD but also the strength and resilience it had created within her.

Lucy explained that in her artwork, she explores how she felt lost in her OCD. In Figure 1.4, you can see that she painted the feeling of losing herself in the overwhelming nature of OCD and how it can totally exhaust her with repetitive thoughts. She then said that by painting and drawing, she has been able to understand, visually, what is happening for her.

Believe it or not, our rocks can be celebrated. They might make us stronger, more independent, empathic, smarter, and creative—if not right now, then possibly in the future.

Lean in When Kids Act Out

This chapter has been about restorying our students, viewing them in new ways, and helping them view themselves in new ways. We want to conclude this first chapter with an analogy from Josh Shipp (2015), an expert on supporting kids with challenging behavior and the adults those kids can challenge. Shipp begins the

Figure 1.4: Lucy's Rock

Source: Artwork by Lucy Benton. Reprinted
with permission.

analogy by asking you to remember the last time you rode a roller coaster and the
safety bar came down over your lap. You probably tested the bar by shaking it, hard,
before the ride began. But you didn't test the safety bar because you hoped it would
fail and you'd go plummeting to your death as soon as the first upside-down loop
appeared. You tested the safety bar to *confirm* its stability, ensure it was safe and
secure, and confirm its ability to protect you.

Shipp explains that this is exactly what kids are doing when they challenge
us. Kids with challenging behaviors have significant uncertainty in their lives.
Remember all those rocks they are carrying around? All those skills they still need
to learn? All those feelings of belonging and safety they crave and perhaps don't
have yet? When they test you with behaviors, they are simply looking to you to
confirm that *you* are stable, certain, and safe. Therefore, the next time a kid tests
you, we want you to simply be the safety bar for them. Know that they are simply
confirming you are there for them, no matter what. Don't push them or send them
away when they challenge you. Lean in.

Tiny To-Do List

☐ Use your journal to complete any exercises in this chapter.

☐ Take five minutes and write a new story about a specific student.

   ☐ What are this student's strengths, gifts, and talents?

   ☐ What are some possible reasons for their behavior(s)?

☐ Write down one thing you can do today to build confidence in a student who is struggling and one thing you can do to lean in and provide them with the certainty they are seeking. Implement those new actions as soon as you can.

Focusing on Educators' Mental Health:
Developing Love and Self-Care

One of the very best things you can do to support kids with challenging behavior is to promote your own health, happiness, and well-being by establishing a daily practice of self-love and self-care. Many of us feel that taking time for ourselves simply cannot happen, isn't practical, or isn't logistically feasible. But we believe that everything in this book depends on making yourself a priority. There are many dominant discourses in schools that need to be disrupted in order to increase the health of the system, which is dependent on the health of each and every individual educator. In this chapter, we provide ways of thinking (i.e., habits of mind) and ways of being (i.e., specific practices and strategies) to improve the mental health of educators. First, we will cover the intangibles.

Maybe you already take excellent care of yourself, eat right, exercise, and have people and activities in your life that fill you up emotionally and spiritually. If that is the case, feel free to read on to see if you can simply increase your self-care. But if you are like many educators, self-care might not currently be on the top of the list. Soon, we hope, you will understand the need for self-care as a daily practice so you can be the educator you want to be for all the kids, especially those who challenge you.

Imagining What a Full Cup Feels Like

When our emotional, physical, cognitive, and spiritual cup is full, it is easier for us to share our time, knowledge, and love with others. When our cup is full, we have the presence of mind and energy to give to others, our patience levels are higher, and we can function better for ourselves and our students. Alternatively, when we are depleted, exhausted, and running on empty or solely on caffeine, we can be short-tempered, short on presence, and short on exactly what our students need from us—our positive attention, energy, and love.

It is our dream for all educators to have full, overflowing cups. Educators who are rested and in the right emotional and physical space can support all students with love and kindness. Supporting all students requires intense levels of energy, presence, and patience. But working with students who have challenging behavior can feel very personal and emotionally taxing.

Examining How We Talk to Ourselves

First, a few personal questions: How do you talk to yourself? What are the typical things you say to yourself? Is it kind and compassionate, or is it full of judgment and critique? We know that, as humans, we are more likely to dwell on the negatives than the positives in our life; we are most often our own worst critics. Instead of criticizing yourself, what would it sound like to talk to yourself with love and compassion? What would it sound like if you were your own biggest and best supporter?

Let's try a scenario to gauge where you currently are with your self-talk. You are running late for a meeting or you just missed an important deadline. Take a moment to consider what you are most likely to say to yourself. Are your words kind and compassionate? Harsh and critical? If they're the latter, we feel you, as do so many others.

If your default is to be unkind to yourself, we want you to focus on turning your self-talk around. Shifting from a mindset of "I'm late, as usual" to "I'm doing my best" isn't easy or quick, but it can be done through consistent, positive self-affirmations. This is important because how we talk to ourselves has a major effect on how we feel. When you coach yourself to respond in kind and compassionate ways to your own actions and feelings throughout the day, you are more likely to feel empowered, calm, and ready to work with students with the most difficult behaviors. Try the affirmations in Figure 2.1. You can also create your own list of affirmations that work best for you.

Figure 2.1: Positive Affirmations

I've got this.	I will treat myself gently right now.
I enjoy learning new things.	All is well right now.
I am always improving.	Day by day, I will improve.
Now here is a challenge.	I trust myself to get through this.
I am a good person.	I am courageous.
I am prepared for this.	I have lots of choices and can decide what to do here.
I am doing a great job.	
Today is going to be amazing.	I will be easy on myself here.
I am doing my best right now.	I am evolving.
I have so much to be proud of.	I trust my capabilities.
I am relaxed.	I am going to look for the positive here.

Recognizing How We Talk to Others

As we walk through the schools in which we work, we often greet our colleagues by asking, "How are you doing?" In response, we hear phrases such as, "I'm busy," "I'm overwhelmed," "I'm under water," "I'm barely alive," or "I'm just surviving." It is not uncommon to hear many nonexamples of self-care in a school. For example, many of our colleagues may say things such as, "I was up grading until midnight," "I ate Cheetos for dinner," or "I brought the baby to school this weekend."

No doubt, educators at some point will feel or do all these things. Many of us feel we are facing what can sometimes feel like untenable challenges. But in some schools, being overwhelmed has nearly become a competitive sport, a culture, or a way of thinking. We call this way of thinking the Overwhelm Olympics, and we know some educators are unknowingly competing. You might even know a colleague who is winning the gold medal in these Olympics. Maybe you earned the gold last week. We suggest not competing in these games at all. This way of thinking will make you feel more tired, overwhelmed, depleted of your mental and physical resources, and will almost always affect your colleagues and students.

We ask you to consider how you might practice a new competitive sport: the Self-care Marathon. The next time someone asks you how you are doing, consider ways you can answer honestly while still infusing energy and positivity because you know this self-care marathon has only just begun. Maybe your response is as simple as "I'm happy to see you and the students." Or maybe it's as enthusiastic as "I had the most energizing weekend!" Or if your go-to response is humor, play around with clever responses that get a laugh and lift someone's spirits. As you begin to think about giving up the Overwhelm Olympics and joining the Self-care Marathon, we want you to consider a few phrases that might come naturally to you when someone asks, "How are you today?" Write a few ideas in your journal.

Evaluating How We Spend Our Time

We communicate our energy and moods through language, but it is also important to look at how we spend our time. If you analyze your schedule closely, it can tell you quite a bit about how you prioritize your time. Do you value meetings, family time, or exercise? Or are you simply on a day-to-day survival plan? Do you have time on the weekend to do things that fill your cup? Take a moment to consider these questions and whether you feel your intentions and values truly match up with your time expenditure. If they don't, we want to help you put some new practices in place.

To begin, we've provided a short list of values in Figure 2.2 that might speak to you. Circle those values that align with your own values and intentions. Then write down any additional values that come up for you, too.

Creating a Culture of Self-Care and Care for Others

Fill Your Cup First

When your metaphorical cup is full, what does it feel like? It might feel like satisfaction, comfort, and winning at life. When your cup is full, you might feel rested, happy, and patient. When our cups are empty, quite the opposite is true. We feel tired, depressed, and short-fused. To determine what actually fills your cup, use Figure 2.3 to pause and think through the concept. Circle any of these experiences, people, or self-care rituals that fill you up and help you feel happier and content.

Figure 2.2: Understanding Your Values

Circle the words that align with your personal values.	
Respect	Equality
Independence	Trust
Friendship	Kindness
Reliability	Justice
Assertiveness	Hard Work
Fun	Honesty
Adaptability	Love
Humility	Gratitude
Community	Self-compassion
Open-mindedness	Patience
Intimacy	Humor

Add additional values that ring true for you:

_____

_____

_____

_____

_____

_____

Plan to Prioritize Your Needs

Select at least one of the things from the list or drawings you created to fill your own cup and make a plan of action. How can you systematically put more of what you need into your life or daily experience? How can you shift your emotions and levels of energy away from feelings of scarcity and sadness and toward feelings of balance, support, and happiness?

Who will you involve to be your self-care sponsor? Finally, write down your plan to increase self-love and self-care each day.

Figure 2.3: Filling Your Cup

Getting enough sleep	Spending time with friends
Eating right	Spending time with family
Honoring quiet time	Hanging out with good colleagues
Engaging in regular exercise and movement	Finding a hobby
Reading	Playing sports
Practicing yoga or stretching	Going to church, synagogue, or mosque
Organizing and tidying up	Doing absolutely nothing
Honoring spirituality or meditation	Doodling
Creating art	Daydreaming
Knitting	Writing
Journaling	Playing music or singing

Use the space below to draw or write about what else might fill your cup:

_____

_____

_____

_____

_____

_____

Transform Your Gratitude

When we look for the positive in any situation, our moods begin to transform. If you open any book about happiness, you will find an entire chapter devoted to gratitude. Many happiness researchers consider gratitude to be the number one happiness booster. If you haven't tried it personally, it is a powerful experience and a joy game changer. If you have tried it, we hope you sustain the practice. If you've stopped practicing, recommit.

Write down what you're grateful for every day, in whatever way feels best to you. Ask yourself, "What am I thankful for today?" Your gratitude writing can take many forms, such as the following:

- Writing in a gratitude journal.
- Creating a gratitude sticky note collage.
- Making gratitude drawings.
- Maintaining a gratitude file on your computer.
- Sending a gratitude email to yourself.
- Sharing gratitude texts with friends.
- Creating color-coded and formatted gratitude lists.

Put your gratitude journal by the side of your bed and create a nighttime ritual. You can choose to write before or after school. You can take on practicing yoga or meditation before writing to spend some time thinking about all you have to be thankful for. Dedicate a gratitude partner and send notes of gratitude to each other before turning off your devices and going to sleep.

Share the Love with Reflective Compliments

For many years, we have been leading reflective compliment circles in schools in dozens of ways. Reflective compliments are any written note that is given to a specific person for the purpose of thanking them, connecting to them, and lifting their spirits by showing them that we see them and value them for who they are. We have seen several variations of the reflective compliment used over the years.

One principal writes one for each staff member on the first Friday of the month. Another school takes the first five minutes of each staff meeting and has each teacher stop and write two reflective compliments and deliver them to the people in the room. A middle school principal takes time during the full faculty meeting to have teachers write a reflective compliment to their classes. In another school, the entire staff wrote reflective compliments to give to a retiring superintendent in what we called a "compliment shower." The staff lined up and each gave her their compliment, a hug, or handshake. Another teacher takes time each day to notice and write five new compliments and share them with other staff members.

There are countless ways to use a reflective compliment, so we ask you to use them in any way that works for you. Nothing creates a community of caring quite like having adults notice and comment on the incredible work of one another.

A 5th grade teacher wrote the following note to the custodian who greets students in the morning: "I have noticed how welcoming you are to every single student and parent in the morning as you greet people. You not only make them each feel special, but it makes me feel inspired to see you each morning. I am proud to work with someone who tends to our community so carefully. Thank you!"

After handing his note to the custodian and connecting with her with a smile, the teacher said he felt good all day as he remembered the interaction. He was motivated to continue sharing reflective compliments because of the impact it had on him and the other person. Not only does gratitude boost the mood of a colleague or friend, you also receive a happiness recharge through the excitement of giving to others.

Community Matters

Building your community of like-minded educators is another important element of supporting your own health and well-being. Health research tells us that when we feel a sense of belonging and trust, we are likely to be healthier. When we feel a greater connection to our community, we are more likely to implement practices that will improve our own mental and physical health, as well as those of others (Carman et al., 2016). Community support can help you build new habits and ways of moving and thinking in the world. They can also help you sustain your momentum and good work.

One example we love came to us from the suburbs of central New York. Frau Shore, a high school German teacher, created what she calls a Zen Teachers group. Her group includes seven other teachers from the school, and together they have committed an hour a week to learn from global masters of mindfulness, wellness, and education. They read selected books, watch TED talks and documentaries, and take online courses. Then they get together before or after school, or occasionally on a weekend at someone's home, to discuss how to bring the learning and practices into their own lives and into the lives of their school community. Frau Shore explains that this purposeful group has changed her life for the better and has helped her bring mindfulness and self-care practices into her students' lives as well.

Understanding That Movement Is Necessary

The research on exercise and happiness is clear. People who get 30 minutes of exercise per day are happier and healthier than those who don't (Zhang & Chen, 2019). Although these findings may not initially make us feel happy, let's talk about what you can do to promote more play and movement for yourself and your students in school.

Get outside and play. Gina, a middle school teacher we know, skips her planning time on Fridays to join her students in the gym or outside recess area. On Fridays, the students usually play a group game or sport, so she joins in on a team. She rotates and engages with different students each week so she can connect more deeply with all of them throughout the year. In addition, she gets exercise and boosts her happiness and health. When they play, she and her students laugh, joke, and build trust and deeper connections that positively influence their relationships both in and out of the classroom.

Make collaboration active. Instead of sitting through another meeting, stand, stretch, or take it on the road for a walking meeting.

Move rather than lounge. Put a treadmill or a rebounder in the staff lounge. Create a way you can get your energy going again instead of sitting and having food that might make you feel sluggish and guilty.

You pick. Think about ways to get moving that make you smile and laugh. In fact, stop reading now and go for a run, jump on your children's trampoline, take a walk or hike, ride a bike, practice yoga, take a dance class, or go for a swim.

All of us, not just those who are kinesthetically inclined, require movement to increase our mental and physical health. Sitting for extended periods of time in order to create lesson plans, write IEPs, and the 101 other tasks we need to accomplish for our students and school communities are all difficult on our bodies and minds. We know all too well that when we aren't running around schools and working with educators, we are often writing and sitting for hours in our office. If we forget to set our 15-minute timers to tell us when it's time to get our move on (i.e., stretching, lunging, or even jumping on a mini-trampoline), we can feel cranky and unmotivated.

Making Fun a Little Bit Brainy

There is substantial research across disciplines that provides evidence that fun improves behavior and learning for ourselves and our students. Brain research suggests that fun is beneficial to learning because fun increases dopamine, endorphins, and oxygen, which encourages motivation for and retention of learning (Willis, 2007). Several reports found that positive emotions can produce increased academic achievement and authentic learning (Um, Plass, Hayward, & Homer, 2012), including retention and long-term memory (Tyng, Amin, Saad, & Malik, 2017). When we are in positive emotional or physical states, we trigger optimal brain activation. We feel positive when we can connect material to our personal life or interests, when learning is presented in an interesting or exciting way, when our curiosity is piqued, or even when we are simply laughing and playing with others (Willis, 2007).

One community-based study about fun and motivation we love is from Volkswagen's Fun Theory Initiative (2009). Volkswagen's Fun Theory website explains that it is "dedicated to the thought that something as simple as fun is the easiest way to change people's behavior for the better." To put this theory to test, Volkswagen designed and built a musical staircase at the Odenplan subway station in Stockholm, Sweden. When pressure was applied to a stair, it played a musical note. They asked the following question: "Can we get people to take the stairs instead of the escalator if the stairs are fun?" The resulting video shows that more commuters chose the fun "piano stairs" over the escalator. On the day the video was filmed, the musical steps successfully motivated 66 percent more people to use the stairs over the escalator. More proof that fun, engaging activities can motivate us to do something new and behave in a new way.

Boosting Your Own Mood in the Classroom

When you are prepared for the day and have exciting and fun lessons planned, how do you feel? How you infuse more play and fun in your own classroom depends mainly on your personality. For example, some teachers may have students bring in jokes, play pranks, or create a spirit of fun in the classroom. Others may crank up the tunes for the occasional dance party. Some teachers may turn learning into creative games while others bring in a short YouTube clip that connects to each lesson. Each of these ideas makes learning fun for students and can be a little bit of self-care for you, too.

We know from research and our own experience that the biggest predictors of happiness are not things like money or career success. Instead, happiness is based on optimism, deep social connections, and a mindset that things can get better and that anything is possible.

You are the basis of all your relationships, experiences, and effective teaching skills. We want you to take a few moments to think carefully about how you are feeling, both in the micro and macro sense. How do you feel today, and how do you feel in general? Do you feel fulfilled, balanced, stressed, satisfied, happy, anxious, or relaxed? Something else? Hold on to your answers while you read about the groovy and research-based ideas in the next section that should help you boost your own happiness.

Reflecting Happiness

Three things we know from happiness researchers such as Shawn Achor (2010) and Gretchen Rubin (2009) are that

1. Happiness is a choice.
2. Happiness can spread.
3. Happiness can give you an advantage.

When we meet our own needs, we are more likely to enrich and enliven everyone we come across, including our students. We believe that if you are more fulfilled, happier, balanced, and calm, your students will be happier, and your classroom will be a more loving and balanced place to learn. Take time to answer the following questions for yourself. Consider your own personal happiness. You can write, draw, or simply state the answers to yourself.

- When was the last time I really laughed?
- Where do I feel deprived?
- What do I need more of to be happier?
- What do I need less of to be happier?
- What does happiness look, feel, taste, and smell like?
- Am I optimistic or pessimistic most of the time?
- To increase my own happiness, I really need _____.
- What am I yearning for?
- What am I starving for?
- What is causing me to feel resentful? Why?
- What brings me joy, makes me smile, or makes me chuckle?
- What makes me howl with laughter?

Now cultivate more happiness and self-care in your personal life by allowing space for more. What might you need to schedule more or less of? What might you need to ask a friend to support you with?

Creating a Reflective Healing Practice

This section is for you to reflect on each day and provide you with a process for healing the challenging emotions that come from this very difficult work of teaching.

Reflect on a difficult situation with a student. Follow these steps to help transform your relationship with the situation. Begin to heal yourself so you can also heal the situation:

Step 1: Describe the situation in full detail.

Step 2: Describe your feelings about the situation. You can use this list of feelings to get you started: anxiety, fear, panic, sadness, anger, embarrassment.

Step 3: Where do those feelings live or reside inside your body?

Step 4: Describe a time you have felt like this before.

Step 5: At that time, what did you need? What did you need to hear? What did you not receive when that type of situation arose in the past? For example, I needed comfort from my mom. I needed her to help and say it would all be OK.

Step 6: What would it look like to give yourself that exact thing now?

Reflect Daily

Every day, we want you to set your intentions for self-care. Ask yourself, "What will I do that will fill my cup? What can I schedule in my calendar that will increase my own happiness and well-being? With whom do I want to connect today? What are the biggest and most powerful levers I can pull in order to make a big difference in my own levels of happiness and mental health?"

Give Yourself Permission to Commit

Self-care and self-compassion need to be strengthened and practiced daily in order to meet the demands of supporting all learners, especially the challenging ones. If you notice, we put this chapter early in the book because we see it as deeply foundational to the work of supporting kids who challenge us. You can only be loving and compassionate with others when you practice love and compassion for yourself regularly. We hope you return to this important topic again in order to continue to become your happiest, healthiest self.

Tiny To-Do List

- ❒ Complete the exercises in this chapter.
- ❒ Practice kind and compassionate self-talk.
- ❒ Cultivate more happiness and self-care in your personal life by starting small with one new activity or practice this week.
- ❒ Share the love. Give someone a gratitude note or reflective compliment this week. Maybe you can give it to the student who is challenging you the most.

Belonging:
Putting Your Love on Display

Julie's Story of *Bibimbap* and Belonging

After working in a middle school all day, I went to my favorite Korean restaurant near my home and sat down at my usual table by the window. Helen, the owner, came over and gave me a hug. She loudly and playfully asked, "Where have you been?" We started talking about her summer plans, her daughter's cold, her new favorite grocery store, and my upcoming wedding. Then we shifted the subject to the task at hand, ordering my meal. "The usual?" she asked. "Bibimbap, no sprouts? Add spicy mayo? Any tea today?" I nodded and she returned with my tea and water. Each time she stopped by the table, we would continue our conversation.

As I sat there waiting, I surprised myself with a huge, unintentional sigh. I sheepishly looked around and wondered if anyone heard. What was that? I noticed my body had just relaxed for the first time that day. As I drank my tea, basking in the warmth of our conversation and the smell of garlic wafting out of the kitchen, I thought, *I love this place.* Then I thought about why I loved it. I loved the Korean food, but what else did I love? I loved the feeling of belonging. I loved being recognized, seen, and even missed when I didn't stop in. I loved that we connected about new life events and how Helen made me feel known and remembered. It felt like she cared enough to know my preferences and dislikes. It felt like I belonged here. I felt safe, and it felt like home. Helen is a smart restaurant owner, and making her customers feel good is a great strategy. But I think it is more than strategic. I see her genuinely connect with every person who comes into the restaurant. During this particular visit, at the end of the meal, Helen stopped by with a new Korean candy. "I saved you this," she said. "I know you will like it." I tried it, and it was delicious. But even more, her gesture of going a little above and beyond made me smile. It was just one more way for her to say, "I was thinking of you and wanted to share something." We chatted more as I got up to leave, and I told her, "I will see you soon." I meant it because I couldn't wait to come back.

As I drove home, I was still thinking about the feeling of belonging. My mind shifted to the middle school I was working in that week. I wondered if students at the school felt that sense of belonging when they walked through the doors.

I was working in this school because of a particular student, Jeremiah. He was becoming increasingly disruptive, his behavior was generally deteriorating the longer he was in any class, and he left gym or art class almost daily, uttering a loud string of profanity about how stupid or dumb the teacher or the class was. The profanity had gotten more significant, and the school had received six different phone calls that week from parents of other students who overheard his inappropriate rants and were concerned.

In addition, Jeremiah refused to take off his sweatshirt hood and had been wearing the same sweatshirt for the better part of two months. He was getting into more trouble outside school as well and was involved in a recent incident with the police. The school team wanted to do some problem solving about his behavior with me. I observed him for two days and learned many more details from the staff about Jeremiah.

I discovered that Jeremiah never removed his sweatshirt because it was the only item he had from his dad, who passed away nine months before. He became incredibly upset when his sweatshirt had to be washed. He had experienced trauma, and I wondered, does he feel welcomed, seen, and safe at school? If not, what would it take to help him feel that way? What might help Jeremiah feel known and remembered? What if we could create an experience for him to feel like we are doing something special, just for him?

Take a moment to reflect. Think of a place that makes you feel warm and welcome. Describe that place in detail. What makes it feel comfortable and safe?

What would it take to create a school that matched those descriptions? How can we increase the sense of belonging for students in our schools?

In this chapter, we discuss the structures and practices in traditional schooling that can impede a sense of belonging for many of our students. These include pullout programs for students with disabilities and English language learners and separate classrooms for students with behavior challenges. We contrast these traditional practices with more inclusive structures and practices that foster a sense of belonging and deep connections to peers and teachers.

Belonging and the Brain

The frontal cortex is considered to fully develop much later than we initially thought (Sapolsky, 2017). This is important when we think about student behavior because the frontal cortex is responsible for skills like planning for the future, decision making, attention span, and inhibition. It is possible that we may be expecting things from students that they simply cannot do yet.

In Robert Sapolsky's book *Behave* (2017), he references several studies that show what happens in the human brain when young people are rejected, even if the rejection only occurs in a computer simulation and not real life. In sum, Sapolsky explains that physiological rejection hurts adolescents more than adults or younger children. Simultaneously, these studies also found that adolescents have an even stronger need to fit in than younger children or adults. The frantic need for adolescents to belong is so important for us as educators to understand and approach with love and compassion. Let's consider the following example with Kavon.

There's Been a Mistake!

Kavon is an African American middle school student who had been educated in separate settings for students with behavioral challenges from kindergarten through 5th grade. For six years, he was taught in a separate special education program with other students with significant behavioral challenges. Kavon often withdrew and refused to do work. During 3rd and 4th grade, when he would refuse to do something, he would repeatedly yell, "I hate this stupid class. I'm just one of the stupid kids and I don't want to do that stupid work!"

The special education teacher in the behavior program during those years shared, "Kavon was often restrained. As he got older and stronger, restraining him got more difficult. Often times, he was very angry about school and how he felt about himself." When we asked Kavon's mother about his years spent in the separate special education program, she said, "Every year, the school said, 'Kavon would be best served in the small special education room.' I asked how is his *behavior* going to improve if he spends all his time with other kids who also don't behave? I like the teachers and trust their professional opinion about him, but putting him all day only with other naughty kids . . . that never made sense to me."

His Individualized Education Program (IEP) entering 5th grade labeled him with emotional disturbance and described him as a student who could not benefit from instruction in the general education environment. Other descriptors on Kavon's IEP included issues with truancy, low self-esteem, continual outbreaks in class, crying, anger issues, disruptive behavior, and refusal behavior.

According to the district administrator, Kavon would likely have continued to be educated in segregated settings for the remainder of his K–12 schooling experience. This was the pattern for a majority of students in this district who were placed in separate special education classrooms, but the school district adopted a more inclusive philosophy and worked to shift their service delivery models to align with philosophies of inclusion. They created a three-year plan for this shift. As a part of this three-year inclusive reform plan, when Kavon entered 6th grade, the separate behavior program had been dismantled. According to the principal, they had decided that the continuum of special education services was to be provided in a collaborative and inclusive manner.

Therefore, in 6th grade, Kavon was part of a general education class, and his special education services were brought to him. The principal explained their revised service delivery as follows: "Special education teachers were team planning and coteaching [on average] between two general education classrooms. In Kavon's case, there were lots of individual accommodations and individualized aspects of that planning, but in general, his special education teacher spent about half the day in his classroom and when she wasn't there, there was usually a [para-professional.]"

In preparing for the new year and new service delivery, collaborative teams of general and special education teachers received two and a half days of time to begin their planning and develop their team. Part of each day was facilitated to get teams to know one another and establish working norms, but part of the time was left for teams to plan and get ready for the coming year. During that professional development time, Kavon's general education teacher said, "I am pretty excited for this change. I am not sure what we are getting into, but I see the merit in having all of our students as part of regular classroom communities and working on grade-level curriculum." Kavon's special education teacher was much more hesitant. "I know we will try our best, but some kids . . . just need different things than what happens in regular classrooms."

The first day of school in his new general education class, Kavon's teacher reported that he was well-behaved, motivated, and participated eagerly. Yet at the end of the day, he sat at his desk and put his sweatshirt hood over his head. As all the other students were lining up to go home, Kavon refused to get up and would not look at his teacher. She recognized this type of refusal behavior from his IEP. She went up to him and asked him what was wrong.

"I'm afraid there's been a mistake," he responded. The teacher asked him what he meant. He said, "I have never been in a class like this."

Kavon told her that he was afraid if he went home, the school would figure out the mistake that he had been placed in the wrong class. He was afraid that he'd have to go back to the class for "bad kids." The teacher then explained that the whole class, including Kavon, was going to work very hard this year, but there was no mistake. He was in the right classroom.

Reflecting on this change, Kavon's mother discussed both her excitement and apprehension. She said,

> I was worried about Kavon being in the regular classroom because he had been in the small room for all the other grades. The school had always said he needed to be in that small room; that [the separate special education room] would be better for his behavior. So when we talked about this change at his [IEP] meeting, I was nervous. I liked that he would be in a regular class, and I liked that he would make new friends and get to do all the things that 6th graders would get to do, but, you know, the school had always told me he needed to be in that small room, and now it was like they were telling me they were wrong about that because they wanted him in the regular grade. I felt confused. I was excited for him, but I was confused about why the change.

She shared that she had always had a lot of communication with the teacher in the self-contained special education classroom. The communication was mostly about how "naughty" Kavon was. She stayed in regular contact with his teachers as he moved into a general education classroom, and the teachers always tried to find ways to give Kavon leadership roles, from small duties around the classroom to bigger roles like nominating him for the principal advisory council. Kavon appeared to thrive. In revisiting his IEP late in the fall of 6th grade, several new descriptors were added about Kavon that were not present in previous IEPs. These descriptions included the following: "He often sits in the car early for school"; "He doesn't want to be late"; "He hasn't missed a day of 6th grade"; "He is eager, participatory, funny, and has made many friends"; and "He is a leader and a stellar community member." Kavon's mother shared that he had been invited to two birthday parties by kids from his class and was very excited to go to both of them. She also noted that he often played with other kids from his class after school and on weekends.

In the spring of 6th grade, Kavon was exited from special education. His teachers, the special education administrator, and Kavon's mother agreed he no longer qualified for special education. Kavon's general education teacher was clear that "Kavon still has behavioral challenges and has many difficult days, but his struggles and refusals are not more extreme than other kids in the grade." Exiting special education was a dramatic shift for a student who had spent the first six years of his education in separate classes. Given how decades of research have demonstrated that school behavior of African American boys is seen, labeled, and reacted to in harsh and radicalized ways, we wonder if Kavon's label of emotional disturbance was misguidedly influenced by that context. Had he been placed in special education mistakenly? We do not have data to address those important questions, but students in separate settings do not often get exited from special education as they are seen as having significant and severe needs.

At the end of the year, Kavon's general education teacher reflected, "The first day of school, Kavon didn't want to leave because he was sure the school had made a mistake and that we would send him back to the 'stupid' self-contained, special education class. There *had* been a mistake, a *huge* mistake. But that mistake was *not* this classroom. That mistake was the years prior when we had kept him in the special education classroom."

Kavon's schooling experiences were most likely a product of his intersecting identities as an African American, a male, and a student with a label of emotional disturbance. Educational scholars have long documented the disparities and inequities in response to African American boys' behavior. Given the disparate future chances of lower graduation rates, as well as high incarceration rates for African American boys with behavioral challenges (Izzo & Horne, 2016), Kavon's change of placement and subsequent exiting of special education appear to have shifted his educational experience—and potentially his future possibilities. Kavon's mother shared that when he went to middle school, he went on to earn a place on that school's honor roll.

Belonging and the Hierarchy of Needs

Anyone who has taken an introductory psychology course or listened to a podcast about psychology has probably heard of Abraham Maslow's Hierarchy of Needs. It is a five-tier model of human needs most often represented in a triangle drawing. It is typically used as a means to discuss human motivation. The base of the triangle, considered to be most necessary for growth, includes physiological needs such as food, water, warmth, and rest. The second tier is composed of the need for security and safety. The third tier includes the need for belonging, love, intimate relationships, and friendships. The fourth tier takes on our self-esteem needs, which includes feelings of accomplishment. The final area is self-actualization or the desire to become your best self. The goal of human development is to get each student to the concept of self-actualization or the top of the triangle.

Belonging and Schools

Self-worth is created when students begin to achieve mastery, recognition, and respect. Most of us would agree that self-worth is a necessary stepping-stone to self-actualization where students pursue their inner talents and find creative fulfillment. However, in the insightful article *The Need to Belong: Discovering Maslow's Hierarchy of Needs,* author Norman Kunc (1992) suggests that in schools, we have a structure in place that is likely to impede development of self-actualization. He suggests that the very structure of separate special education classrooms or behavior rooms, like those in which Kavon was educated, creates a lack of access to feelings of belonging. The hierarchy of needs is therefore inverted.

This means that our students have had to earn their way in to perform or to have access to meaningful learning. When those stages are inverted, it is nearly impossible for students to reach their full potential.

Pullout Instruction and Belonging

Pullout instruction has long been used for the purpose of remediating deficits in students. Specialists remove a student from the typical instruction for the purpose of intensive instruction. However, it seems that the problems with pullout structures far outweigh the intended benefits.

By contrast, we know through decades of research in hundreds of schools that inclusion in general education is a critical predictor of outcomes within and beyond school (Benz, Lindstrom, & Yovanoff, 2000; Carter & Hughes, 2005; Fisher & Meyer, 2002; Hughes, Cosgriff, Agran, & Washington, 2013; Kurth & Mastergeorge, 2010; Test et al., 2009). We know students do better academically in inclusive settings, and we know challenging behavior decreases. We also understand that inclusive classrooms increase the positive socioemotional learning for students with and without disabilities. Research shows that with appropriate supports and services, inclusion in general education settings can help students with support needs feel a greater sense of belonging and provide them with meaningful access to friendships (Fisher & Meyer, 2002; Ryndak, Alper, Hughes, & McDonnell, 2012) and high expectations (Soukup, Wehmeyer, Bashinski, & Bovaird, 2007). Studies also indicate that students develop a deeper level of acceptance for diversity when educated in inclusive classrooms (Fisher, Pumpian, & Sax, 1998; Krajewski & Hyde, 2000; Morningstar, Shogren, Lee, & Born, 2015).

Despite decades of research that point to the benefits of inclusion, segregated classrooms, programs, and schools continue to be used throughout the country to educate students with disabilities, particularly students with challenging behavior. The most recent Annual Report to Congress on the Implementation of the Individuals with Disabilities Education Act (U.S. Department of Education, 2015) evidenced that in 2015, 37 percent of our students with disabilities served under IDEA are excluded from general education for at least 20 percent of their school day.

Nearly 50 percent of students with labels of emotional disturbance (ED) are excluded from general education classrooms for at least 20 percent of their school day, whereas 35 percent of students with labels of ED are segregated for 60 percent or more of their school day (U.S. Department of Education, 2019, p. 49). Once students from linguistically and culturally diverse groups are labeled, particularly with ED, they are more likely to stay in these segregated placements longer than their white classmates who carry the same disability label (Cartledge, Singh, & Gibson, 2008; U.S. Department of Education, 2019).

With all these data on the benefits of inclusion for all students, and the persistence of exclusion for our students with disabilities, we must ask for whom does the exclusion of our students, particularly those with challenging behavior, serve? We also have to ask, how can we begin to reimagine structures and belonging for our most challenging students?

Using Pullout Instruction

It does not feel good to be removed from your community due to a perceived deficit in learning or expected behaviors. We know because we've experienced it ourselves. We've seen it in schools and in our research. We've even created a simulation of a pullout structure to help educators better understand those feelings.

The Red Dot. In a large ballroom in Milwaukee, Wisconsin, we were facilitating a professional development session on the topic of differentiation. Before educators arrived, we randomly placed red stickers under 12 chairs. As the participants came in, they took their seats around large circular tables. After about an hour of presenting, Julie said, "I have spoken to your administrators and have learned that some of you struggle with differentiation. If you are someone who struggles, there will be a red dot under your chair." Julie made sure to let them know that it was not a problem at all if they needed this support. She emphasized this by saying, "We are always learning and growing. But if you have a red dot, please stand and go to the back of the room with Kate. She will be leading the small group at a slower pace." Everyone in the ballroom looked surprised. They glanced at one another and began shifting in their seats. Finally, 11 people stood and went to the back of the room with Kate. However, one person who had a dot placed under her chair did not stand. When I approached her with the microphone, I explained that I believed there was a dot under her chair.

"There is not a dot under my chair," she said loudly into the microphone. I bent down and retrieved the dot. I showed it to her.

"Here it is. Perhaps you missed it. Would you please join Kate in the back?"

She looked angry and walked in a huff to the back of the room. The 12 educators, including the huffy woman, missed an hour of the workshop content while they worked slowly through basic differentiation definitions and practice. When Kate eventually brought them back to the larger group, we explained that it was just a pullout simulation and shared that we had not talked to their administrators at all. Their responses were profound.

One teacher who had gone to the small group explained, "Oh god, I knew I would have a red dot because I know I'm not all that good at differentiation yet. But I was just *devastated* to think my administrator thought so and would have to walk in shame to the back of the room."

"I'm just pissed I missed the video [you showed]. How am I going to watch it now?"

"I felt so ashamed walking to the back while everyone else, who apparently are all very good at differentiation, watched me retreat."

An educator who had remained in the large group shared, "I immediately felt superior. I can't believe it, but it's true."

But the huffy teacher did not want to simply raise her hand. She left her seat and walked right up to me and asked for the microphone. I shook my head at first, but she took the microphone from my hand. She stated, "Do you have any idea what it feels like to stand and leave the room because of a perceived deficit? I was mortified and publicly humiliated."

By structuring our learning in the same way many schools structure learning, we created many issues within our educator group. We set up an environment in which teachers doubted themselves and their skills, felt ashamed and judged, and believed they were superior to their peers. This environment also created a behavior issue from the huffy teacher who not only refused to leave but also commandeered the microphone. This type of pullout structure does not create a safe and caring space for learning and belonging, but it often creates challenging behavior.

Separate Classrooms Do Not Create Belonging

Consider, for a moment, the traditional idea that in order to educate students with behavioral challenges, it is best to put them with other students who also have behavioral challenges. Perhaps we put them in one room or maybe in an altogether separate school. This happens all the time for our students with challenging behavior and labels of emotional disturbance and emotional disabilities. But what actually happens when we put students with similar challenges together? Do they learn better? Do they behave better? Do they feel better about themselves? Are their needs really met?

Norman Kunc (1992) challenges the notion of self-contained behavioral programs and classrooms. He explains that if students with behavioral challenges are expected to learn basic skills (e.g., remain quiet in class and follow directions without support) in separate self-contained classrooms *before* they are allowed to enter regular education classrooms, then we are making it nearly impossible for them to succeed. Worse, we are asking those students to prove their worth and that they can belong. Consider this process:

Student → Skills → Regular Classroom

In Kavon's case, we can see that this type of thinking manifested in his special class placement for the first several years of his school career. He had been in a separate setting working on social skills, positive behavior, mediation, task analysis, and responding appropriately to peers. The school, therefore, was requiring Kavon to learn the appropriate skills in order to *earn the right to belong in the regular class*. If it had not been for an entire overhaul in structure and culture within his district and school, Kavon very likely would never have earned his way in.

It is imperative that we flip this way of thinking about our students with challenging behavior. We know that belonging is, in fact, a prerequisite to learning. We also know it is easier to learn skills when students are surrounded by others who already have those skills. People are less likely to learn new skills if they feel ostracized, rejected, and excluded. This is exactly how Kavon felt. You can't learn to belong and learn appropriate social skills while you are systematically isolated and separated. For it is only when we belong that we learn.

Kunc (1992) also argues that the special education practices of the past were founded on the paradigm where skills were the prerequisite to inclusion and belonging. He suggests reversing this order. The challenge therein, however, is to convince educators that we can and should reduce our focus on skills for a short time. This kind of focus would build confidence, belonging, and trust in an inclusive setting for these students. Then we could add in appropriate supports to help develop needed skills. This new process would look like this:

Student → Regular Classroom → Belonging and Trust → Skills with Supports

We expected Kavon to learn how to behave appropriately so he could belong. However, he needed to belong before he could learn the skills with support.

The Circle of Courage

The circle of courage is a positive model of youth development that was initially described in *Reclaiming Youth at Risk* (Brendtro, Brokenleg, & Van Bockern, 2009). This technique was used to explain the complex and respectful child development philosophy and techniques of Native American and First Nation communities. It was used to describe why the "civilizing" techniques in punitive and corrective boarding schools failed. Ultimately, those techniques were in direct opposition to the students' cultural norms. We turn to these ideas to understand this powerful representation of universal growth needs of all children: belonging, mastery, independence, and generosity.

The circle of courage is drawn as a circle because without any one section, the circle will be incomplete and the structure would collapse. Let's look at each of these ideas as they relate to belonging.

Belonging. This core value can be summarized in these simple words: "Be related, somehow, to everyone you know." In this way, all people are drawn to relationships of love and respect. The big concept here is that there is no *other*. Instead, everyone is part of our tribe. Every person is surrounded by relationships of love and trust in order to meet the very human need of belonging.

Mastery. Mastery can occur only when belonging is satisfied. Without belonging, a person cannot achieve mastery of skills. In the Native American and First Nation cultures that were part of the study, children were asked to observe and learn from those who possessed the skill. They were viewed as models, not rivals. Mastery of skills breeds a desire for more skills or motivation.

Independence. Inner discipline is the goal. Therefore, children are encouraged to make decisions, solve problems, and show personal responsibility. The role of the adult is to nurture, give feedback, and teach values. Nevertheless, children were asked to make decisions and learn from those role models. Independence is dependent on the idea of belonging.

Generosity. Virtue here was reflected in the value of generosity. This is the central goal of child rearing, which is to encourage and support children to make positive contributions to another human life. Again, this preeminent value cannot be discovered without a sense of belonging.

Ensuring and Creating Student Connections

The staff at Cold Spring Middle School in Reno, Nevada, wanted to be sure that every student was valued and known in their school. Their philosophy was that their students were people—not pupils. The more they were valued for their individuality, the more they would feel an authentic sense of belonging. This work is steeped in the idea that an individual's sense of belonging can boost achievement.

They first determined how to measure if every student were known by a teacher. They conducted a teacher-student connection poster activity where all the teachers gathered in the library and listed each student on poster paper around the room. The teachers had to identify if they could recognize the student by face, their first and last names, academic information about each student, and in-depth personal information or anecdotes about each student. The key to this activity was to understand which students needed deeper connections with adults.

Next, they developed an action plan around the students who had fewer connections to teachers in the building. Their plans included the following:

- **Thumbs-up Thursdays:** A time for students to share things they are proud of.
- **Feel Good Fridays:** A time for students to share a moment that made them feel happy or successful.
- **Hallway Chats:** Teachers station themselves in hallways for the sole purpose of creating connections with students as they pass from class to class.
- **Greetings:** Teachers began using new greetings to learn more about individual students. For example, a 7th grade science teacher used simple questions like, "What is your favorite fruit?" or "What is your favorite season?" As students walked through the door, they each got a high five as they answered the question. The video of this particular school and these strategies can be found on Edutopia at www.edutopia.org/video/making-sure-each-child-known.

Celebrating Diversity

Research across many disciplines shows that diversity is critical to success. In education research specifically, the scholar Ellen Brantlinger (1997) suggests that "individual and group diversity contributes positively to classroom climate, learning outcomes, and community quality" (p. 435). Other education researchers have highlighted that skills, relationships, and membership in a diverse class community are the three most important domains that contribute to increased participation in culturally valued roles, activities, and settings for students (Schwartz, Staub, & Peck, & Gallucci, 2006).

The goal of inclusion is not to create uniform human beings who are finally valuable enough to belong because they no longer have deficit areas or differences. Often in our society, however, uniformity and perfection are idolized and over-valued. If that statement causes you to pause, consider the standardized test, the standardized classroom, the standard developmental stages, norms of beauty represented in the media, and norms of success and family structures.

Now consider how our goals in education might change if we were focused on valuing the ways students vary in academic performance, behavior, communication styles, life experience, communication and language experience, socio-economic status, race and ethnicity, and countless other ways. It is indeed this beautiful variation that helps us fully experience the awesome wonder of the individual and collective community. Celebrating those differences and supporting students to learn about their individuality is one important step toward creating an inclusive and loving classroom. We think the poet Joshua Bennett (2012), in a poem for his brother Levi, describes this need powerfully in the following words:

> This is not just about my younger brother but our obsession with normalcy and the wars we have waged in its name. . . . Levi, they will come for you too. They will tell you to laugh and lift and work on cue. And if you can't muster the emotion, just fake it like all the other good robots do. Be human, be like me, be a social butterfly with gender normative wings. Smile big, smile pretty. Be quarterback, point guard, cat-call, courageous, bicep, jackhammer, spark. Your scribbles are just scribbles Levi, don't dare call them art. Don't dare be an enigma, there is no room for your kind of beautiful here. (Watch him perform the full poem at https://www.youtube.com/watch?v=zoAXfzEU9xU)

We can do better for Levi and for all students. Let us be the ones to make room for all kinds of beautiful.

Learning from the *I Am Norm* Campaign

There are many ways to redefine normal and to celebrate diversity. One initiative we love came from Dan Habib's groundbreaking film *Including Samuel* (2007), which seeks to promote inclusion and redefine the word *normal*. Students all over the country hosted showings of the film in their communities. Communities also used the nametag shown in Figure 3.1 with their students. Several teenagers then got together for a summit to develop an advocacy campaign focused on the following:

- Raising awareness about inclusion through a viral video campaign and website.
- Providing opportunities for youth and adults to share their ideas about inclusion.
- Promoting inclusive practices in schools and community organizations.

If you are interested in bringing the *I Am Norm* campaign to your school, visit www.IamNorm.org and connect with your students to make it a reality.

Put Your Love on Full Display

There are many different ways to create an authentic sense of belonging in schools. Lastly, for one last sweet tidbit, we want to show you a school system that keeps its lights on after school and on weekends, primarily for creating a

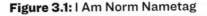
Figure 3.1: I Am Norm Nametag

community of belonging, love, and safety. The principal reports that he knows this type of belonging has actually saved lives.

West Side High School principal Akbar Cook had lost many students to gun violence, gang violence, and crime. He noticed that most of these incidents occurred outside school on Fridays, between the hours of 6 p.m. and 11 p.m. He turned the lights on in the school on Friday nights and invited adults and students into the building. He provided excellent food, such as jerk chicken, curry chicken, and macaroni and cheese; hosted makeup artists and nail techs; and created spaces to play video games and dance to music curated by a DJ.

Akbar's core plan was to bring students in, connect to those students who may have been feeling lost, grieving, or in pain, and give them conversation, activities, and a warm and caring atmosphere to simply be. Students report that every Friday, they come to the building for that love, food, and connection. This should be the new norm for education. We can make sure there is light in their lives. Our kids can't wait for new policies that will turn the light on for them. Akbar said that he was hired partly to be principal at West Side High School because he is a large black man. He said he was expected to be a tough drill sergeant type of leader to get students in line. Instead, he realized, "I had to put my love on full display." And he did.

Tiny To-Do List

❐ Complete the reflection exercise in this chapter.

❐ Take a close look at the practices in your school that create division between and among students. List them here. Think of three steps you could take to make those practices more inclusive.

❐ Take three minutes to watch a video about Principal Akbar and West Side High School: https://www.facebook.com/watch/?v=1436949793095826

Creating a Culture of Inclusion

In this chapter, we ask you to look at the ways in which students learn and how to help teach for and embrace diversity in many ways in your classroom. We review how, as educators, what we do and present in our classrooms (i.e., providing and enhancing instruction, curriculum, language, materials, and community) has a significant impact on student behavior and how they feel about themselves, their peers, and you. We share many practices we love that educators can use to decrease challenging behavior, build greater relationships with students, and create a culture of inclusion.

Fill Their Mental Resources

Researchers in psychology and neuroscience have realized that all humans need the following three mental resources in order to survive and thrive: safety, satisfaction, and connection. We particularly like the language psychologist and author Rick Hanson (Hanson & Hanson, 2018, p. 62) has used to define these resources:

- **Safety:** being on your own side, determination, grit, sense of agency, feeling of being protected, clarity about threats, calm, relaxation, peace
- **Satisfaction:** gratitude, gladness, pleasure, accomplishment, clarity about goals, enthusiasm, passion, motivation, aspiration, feeling of enough-ness, contentment

- **Connection:** compassion for others and oneself, empathy, kindness, self-worth, skillful assertiveness, forgiveness, generosity, love

If you are conscious of the fact that all of us need these resources and need to work on building these up throughout our lives, then you can put this mentality to work when you are in the classroom with your students. When you commit to building a classroom culture that first and foremost attempts to meet these three mental needs for your students, you can create a space in which students feel protected and calm in their surroundings, accomplished, grateful, motivated by the work, compassionate, kind, and loving to themselves and others.

Next, you want to provide students with tools and experiences to teach them that they too can commit to filling themselves with these mental resources. By doing this work, you will get your students to a place where they can learn the content you are hoping to teach, as well as help them grow the strengths and mental resources they need.

The Science of Learning

When humans learn, we change the neural structure or function in our brains. Whenever we are teaching students and they truly learn, we are changing their brains. Neuroscience tells us that these changes in neural structure occur in two phases: activation and installation. We must first experience something (e.g., a thought, sensation, dream, or worry) and then install it into our brain's long-term storage. In other words, learning occurs from sustained and repeated experiences.

This means we can only learn compassion, self-worth, confidence, gratitude, strategies for calming our bodies, and how to read, do math, and think critically by having sustained and repeated experiences of all these activities and skills.

In school, students learn so many things, from phonics to electrostatics. It can be easy for us to forget that they also learn kindness, empathy, confidence, and compassion. All of it, however, from phonics to compassion, relies on experience-based neuroplasticity. Having and mindfully internalizing a particular experience, such as feeling valued and confident in a classroom, greatly helps our students more easily evoke those experiences and learnings later in life.

The fun part for us is that once we understand that our students can and do learn skills such as confidence and kindness through sustained and repeated experiences, we get the great joy of purposefully creating opportunities, every single day, for our students to learn those skills.

Rethinking Rules

One of the most significant issues we take with traditional school and classroom rules is that they are often created solely by teachers and administrators. When students are deeply embedded in the process of creating the rules—or as we prefer to call them, class values—they generate ideas that emerge from meaningful conversation about how students really learn, play, and exist together. We believe the process of creating values is the most important part. As Alfie Kohn (2006) puts it,

> There are few educational contrasts so sharp and meaningful as that between students being told what the teacher expects of them, what they are and are not permitted to do, and students coming together to reflect on how they can live and learn together. It is the difference between being prepared to spend a lifetime doing what one is told and being prepared to take an active role in a democratic society (or to transform a society into one that is democratic, as the case may be). (p. 73)

To create a classroom in which students are respected and valued, even when they display challenging behavior, we need to rethink the rules and embrace the concepts of collaboration, creativity, and student voice. Sure, it can be hard for us as educators to embrace the unknown of letting students create their own values and ways of being. An important first step is focusing on building relationships with them. When we provide students with the time, space, and support to create their own class values, they aren't simply sharing ideas they *think* we want to hear; instead, they are sharing from an authentic place because they understand we trust them.

Focusing on Relationships

To create an inclusive environment that reflects our goal of reclaiming the classroom as a place of love, a place that teaches students to grow their mental resources, and a place that creates an environment in which kids know they are trusted and supported, we must consistently connect with our students. When our daily reality is teaching anywhere from 20 to 200 students in a single day, however, we know it can be easy to focus on academics. But this means we are then left to manage and react to behaviors. A systematic review of research (Quin, 2017), however, tells us that it is only when we prioritize building relationships with our students that they can learn and succeed in the classroom. Specifically, we see increased academic achievement, engagement, attendance, and grades, and we see decreased levels of challenging behavior and school drop-out. This is especially true for those students who are more vulnerable and have traditionally been at risk of exclusion or failure in school (e.g., English language learners, students with disabilities), who have experienced trauma, and have challenging behavior.

An important way to create connections with students is to practice empathy. Although empathy is an innate human capacity, it also means we must be open to experiencing and feeling emotions we might not want to feel, particularly when it comes to our most challenging students. And when we practice an empathetic approach with our students, research shows that disciplinary actions decrease—particularly for those who are most at risk (e.g., students of color, students with disabilities, students who have a history of disciplinary action) (Okonofua, Paunesku, & Walton, 2016). We can purposefully and thoughtfully let students know that we love and care about them every day—especially those days when students have recently challenged us with behaviors. Over the years, we've seen wonderful ways that educators have strengthened their abilities to experience and express empathy—and in turn created stronger connections with the students in their care:

- **Share One Thing:** As students settle in to work, have them write, draw, or talk for one minute about something from their day. Listen and respond. Help them know you see them and care.
- **Fist to Five:** Before you begin instruction, ask students to share how they are feeling with a fist to five. A zero or fist says, "I'm feeling pretty bad," and holding up five fingers says, "I'm feeling really great." You can then proceed as needed. If you have a lot of zeroes, maybe you need to take a moment to breathe, watch a funny animal video, or plan for a class meeting.
- **Ask for Input:** Whenever possible, ask students for their ideas—about class values and norms, instructional decisions, or field trips. Then incorporate their feedback into your planning and respond to their ideas and needs.

Relationship Building Actions

Educational research is clear that a positive relationship between teacher and student is one of the most important factors associated with effective instruction and student success. However, students don't always know how we feel about them, particularly if we don't share our feelings often. Your actions, both what you do and say on a daily basis, are crucial to help students understand that you care about them.

Robert Marzano (2011) points out that this can be "liberating" for us. Even if a student challenges us and we are still working toward viewing them through a lens of love, we can interact positively with our words and actions until the student develops the perception of a positive teacher-student relationship. Even if you thought you could never love the student, you likely will find yourself feeling more positively toward them because of the sustained positive interactions. Here are a few relationship building actions we have seen work wonders for student-teacher relationships:

- Tell students they are smart and capable.
- Display student work on the walls.
- Write students letters and positive notes of gratitude.
- Engage students in conversation about their life and interests.
- Help students create positive affirmations for themselves individually and for the whole class, such as "I am enough!" "I am worthy!" "I am loved!" and "I have GOT this!"
- Provide students with ways to shine in class that are purposefully connected to their strengths, talents, and interests (e.g., ask a musical student if they want to be resident DJ during independent work time).
- Attend students' extracurricular activities. Make and bring big, goofy "YOU ROCK" signs.
- Advocate for students in times of need or difficulty.
- Help students catch up on work if they are behind.
- Make time to regularly schedule one-on-one conferences during class.
- Ask a student what his or her theme song might be. Play it loudly one random day when they enter class.

 There are a million other ways we know you can show up for students and build positive relationships with them. We encourage you to take out your journal, jot down all the brilliant ways you are already connecting, and begin to add new ideas to your daily repertoire. In the next section, we share a powerful classwide relationship builder that can change the dynamic of even the most difficult classes: the class meeting.

The Power of Class Meetings

Class meetings—particularly when they're student-directed and focused on sharing, deciding, planning, and reflecting—can be extremely powerful for building relationships and a connected and inclusive classroom community. You can use class meetings to provide students with ways to connect and build class community at the beginning of the year (e.g., creating classroom expectations, arranging classroom furniture, and even brainstorming options for end-of-semester projects). Class meetings can also be used to promote ongoing dialogue and connection about diversity and common interests, problem solving (e.g., discussing a class conflict or how to deal with difficult school, local, national, or world news), planning a field trip or community outreach project or reflecting on class values throughout the year (e.g., asking "Why do we work in collaborative groups?" or "How should we treat one another?").

Class meetings might be as short as 10 minutes or as long as an entire class period, but they are so important and deeply connected to the work of knowing, understanding, and supporting all our students, including those with challenging behavior. Rather than view that precious time as a missed opportunity to teach content, we encourage you to acknowledge the invaluable social, emotional, and intellectual benefits that getting together to talk with your class can bring. Students and teachers find that regular class meetings result in a more positive classroom climate, more motivated and effective learners, increased student responsibility and reasoning skills, and decreased challenging behavior.

Class meetings are often considered an integral part of Restorative Practices (RP). In the context of RP, these meetings are often called connection circles. By engaging in connection circles with students for 30 minutes each week, educators are encouraged to truly build the practice effectively and consistently. Educators at the primary and secondary levels use class meetings and connection circles to build community and relationships with students. And it works.

Kate, Nate, and the High School Connection Circle

Years ago, I had a graduate student, Nate, who was brand new to teaching high school. It was his first year in the classroom, and by November he was completely overwhelmed by the challenging behavior in his 10th grade science classroom. He explained to me that his kids fought with one another, argued with him, left the classroom unannounced, talked through all his lessons, and even called him names.

"They hate me," he said. He was distraught and said, "Maybe teaching isn't for me. Kids don't respect me, and they really don't learn from me. I just don't know how to make them listen or respect me."

Nate and I talked, and I reminded him that teaching is hard and excellent teachers are nothing short of superhumans. I then gently reminded him that it isn't up to us as teachers to make students listen to and respect us. It is up to us, however, to build relationships with our students and value their voices and help them to build a community of respect and love for themselves, one another, and us. Nate admitted that he didn't know if he could build relationships with these students or love them. They were so hard and cruel to him. We talked about a hard-won truth that *love is a practice.* I shared with him that if he took actionable steps toward loving them, he would begin to know their stories, learn about who they really were, what they were working through, and where they were coming from. Then, I explained, it would be nearly impossible not to love his students once he truly knew them. As we talked, I noticed a shift in his thinking about his students' behavior. He began to realize that his students weren't bad or mean; they were communicating to him that something was seriously up. The classroom culture was out of sync, and he, as the educator, was not listening to them or helping them feel connected and safe.

I asked Nate another question: "Do you think your students feel valued? Are their ideas valued in your classroom or in the school or even in the community at large?" This question shook him, because the answer, although he hated to admit it, was *no.* We talked through a few ideas for helping to value students' voices in his class. We landed on his favorite idea—holding class meetings. I then connected him to a colleague of mine who was implementing RP in secondary schools around New York State. The two of them came up with a very specific plan. Nate would hold daily 10–15 minute connection circles with his students, borrowing from the language of RP, and he would use this time to help his students feel heard, open up, and really get to know one another and him. He committed to love as a practice with connection circles as an action step.

Day 1

Nate began by gathering his class together to sit in a circle in the hallway. Nate wanted to change up the setting and the feel, as they had been stuck in a negative rut for the first few months of school. He then explained the purpose as follows: "Our connection circle is a relationship building process so we can better understand one another and share our experiences." Next, Nate shared a few ground rules. He said, "Listen and share with respect. Our verbal and nonverbal language are powerful tools that can help to build each other up. Respect everyone's privacy by only telling your story. Share airtime with one another. Share only when you're holding the talking object, our Koosh ball." He then asked a simple question: "If you could go anywhere this spring break, where would you go and why?"

Days 2–14

Over the next two weeks, Nate continued asking questions that helped the class build relationships with one another, such as "What superhero would you be?" and "What's the best experience you've ever had to date?" He also began to introduce questions during connection circle that were more integrally connected to class content, such as "What is an idea from the unit that you feel you could teach?" "What is something you're still working on?" and "What might be something you have to leave at the door today if you are going to be able to focus on work?"

Nate also alternated the timing of the connection circles. Sometimes, he used them at the beginning of class and sometimes, he ended the class with them. This gave Nate and his students more opportunities to ask new questions and build community in new ways. For example, at the beginning of class, he might ask, "Is there anything you need to do for yourself to get ready for the lab today?" Likewise, at the end of class, he might ask, "Why do you think we had a choice to work in small groups or alone for this particular activity? Was it useful or would you recommend a change?"

Day 25

Five weeks into connection circles, Nate found that not only were they something his students looked forward to, but the challenging behaviors during class were dwindling. Students joked with him. He joked back. He knew some of their stories, and they knew some of his. He realized that by *practicing* love for each of his students, every day, it was much easier to love them—because now he knew how they looked forward to visiting grandparents in Barbados, the rivalries between Mets and Yankees fans, their favorite songs, their fears of heartbreak and cockroaches in the sink. His students also knew, among other things, that he had grown up in Delaware, he played in an adult soccer league, and he had lost his father to cancer when he was only 18. It is safe to assume that the students began to love Nate, too.

Nate is now in his sixth year teaching. He still holds weekly connection circles with all his 11th and 12th graders. He considers himself an activist teacher committed to love, connection, and restorative practices. And let it be celebrated that his students consider him one of the "most real" teachers in the school.

We think Nate's story exemplifies the truth that people are wired to connect. Consciously and unconsciously, we seek connection. When we are faced with difficulty in the classroom, rather than give up on our own capacity to love and connect, we must instead use all the tools available.

Building Friendships with Purpose

As kids continue through middle and high school, their connections grow as a result of shared interests and enjoyment together. When educators use information learned about students' interests to help them connect and foster closeness, friendships, and community, they are practicing love—important work that we believe falls under our job description as educators. Here are a few ways we like to think about purposefully building friendships between and among our students:

- **Valuing friendship:** Provide students with ongoing opportunities to analyze text, music, and films that focus on valuing differences, team building, support, and friendship. In addition to talking about the material, you are encouraging and facilitating conversations about creating supportive, safe, and inclusive classrooms and schools.
- **Literature circles:** Use student-led discussion and literature circles (you can use literature circles in STEM classes, too) to facilitate conversations about content while building connections and friendships from sustained

engagement over the course of the semester. The following strategies are helpful for literature circles:

- Assign students with different roles (e.g., story mapper, reporter, summarizer, word wizard, visual note taker). Consider what strengths students can draw on for their roles. This way, they can be seen as competent and valuable members of the discussion. Remember that participation can look different for everyone.
- Select a range of titles that appeal to different interests and allow students to choose groups and determine reading and meeting schedules.
- Predetermine or work with students to brainstorm how they will document or share reflections (e.g., keeping journals, recording the discussion with videos).

- **Appreciations:** Take time for students to share appreciations of and for one another. This purposeful practice can help all students feel more welcomed and appreciated by peers in specific ways. You can use the following tips for using appreciations:

  - Identify one student each week to sit in the "sweet spot" (i.e., a chair at the front of the classroom). This student gets to hear from a handful of classmates who take turns sharing appreciations for a few minutes.
  - Appreciations can also be woven into curriculum and instruction. Have students practice writing appreciations to one another after collaborative partner or group work.
  - Work on communication or speaking skills with students while giving short appreciation toasts with sparkling water to one another during an end-of-unit celebration.

Cultivating Love and Reliance

Consider the words of Grace Lee Boggs (Boggs & Kurashige, 2012), a civil rights and social activist, author, philosopher, and feminist:

> Imagine what our neighborhoods would be like if, instead of keeping our children isolated in classrooms for 12 years and more, we engaged them in community-building activities with the same audacity with which the Civil Rights Movement engaged them in desegregation activities 50 years ago. Just

imagine how safe and lively our streets would be if, as a natural and normal part of the curriculum from K–12, schoolchildren were taking responsibility for maintaining neighborhood streets, planting community gardens, recycling waste, rehabbing houses, creating healthier school lunches, visiting and doing errands for the elderly, organizing neighborhood festivals, and painting public murals! (p. 158)

As you read Boggs's words, did the ways in which you already connect students with the community come to mind? We are struck by the importance of teaching students about reliance and love for the community. When students learn about reliance, they understand the critical interdependencies and interconnectedness between us all. Here are several ways to intentionally teach reliance in your classroom:

- Scaffold and support students as they are developing and learning, rather than doing the task for them. This can be particularly challenging when we are pressed for time or when you feel like a student really needs to grasp a concept or skill. It is in these moments when students need us to take a step back, give them space and encouragement, and allow them to try it at their own pace. Additionally, we often see challenging behaviors decrease when we approach students this way.

- Provide students with a choice of classroom jobs and tasks they can complete as part of a daily or seasonal routine. This is something that many primary educators do but can be overlooked in secondary classrooms. At both levels, it is important that we provide choice to our students and engage in explicit discussion with the class about why the jobs, tasks, and roles affect the greater good of the class community, the mission of the school, and the students' own health and well-being.

- Teach students the difference between equality and equity. Strive to foster learners who value fairness over sameness and justice over equality. Engage students in conversations or activities regarding these concepts.

- Teach students to rely on one another. We know that peer support is one of the most effective ways to engage students with each other and the content. You can teach students to review content, help with lab set-up, explain directions and instructions, or provide simple adaptations for one another (i.e., prompts or cues). You can also more formally establish reading and math partners, peer mentors, or class or group leaders.

Cultivating Love and Reliance Within the Community for Teachers in Training

Two fabulous learning coaches we know, Jackie and Marissa, started a Teachers-in-Training (TinT) program in their Pennsylvania school district to support community building for students who had challenging behavior. Initially, their program focused on 4th–6th grade students who were communicating through challenging behavior that they needed social, behavioral, emotional, or academic support. Rather than discipline these students for their challenging behaviors, thereby reinforcing a negative cycle of failure and disconnection, Jackie and Marissa knew the students would benefit more from an opportunity to grow positive relationships and leadership skills with their peers and school community. Therefore, they invited several challenging students to participate in an official—but fun—TinT program in which these students would mentor younger students.

During the initial training, Jackie and Marissa emphasized that teachers in training were selected by their teachers for being responsible, hardworking, and kind. They said to the selected students, "You have all the characteristics that our kindergartners need modeled for them." After completing training, which consisted of learning how to support kindergartners in reading, writing, and other academic tasks, students received formal ID badges and certificates and were tasked with helping kindergarten teachers implement cooperative learning stations in their classrooms once a week. When they were in the kindergarten classrooms, the students were called by their official teacher in training names: Mr. or Miss and their last names.

Jackie and Marissa knew that even if it wasn't always going to be smooth sailing, the TinT program was an important responsibility for students and would not be taken away from them due to any continued challenging behavior in their grade-level classrooms. Jackie and Marissa explained it to us this way:

> For some flawed reason, in education, our first response to misbehavior is often to take away the things that matter *most* to students. So when one student asked us during training, "What happens if I get ISS [in school suspension]?," we knew our belief that TinT participation could not be taken away. We decided then and there that ISS or not, TinTs would help in their kindergarten classrooms. (personal communication, June 24, 2019)

At the beginning of the program, Jackie and Marissa provided plenty of support for the TinTs, ensuring there were several adults on hand to help students learn how to redirect the kindergartners, reinforce expectations of their roles, and help avoid any loss of instructional time in the kindergarten class. As the program continued, Jackie and Marissa said what they witnessed was much more than they could ever have imagined:

> We noticed a *physical* difference in our Teachers in Training. These same students who had been so negative, angry, unmotivated, and downright resistant to work, school, and teachers were showing up to school proud, confident, happy, and smiling. Unprompted, the TinTs were taking *data* during their work supporting kindergarten learning stations. They came to us to share which sight words kindergartners were struggling with and which numbers they missed while counting. And the best part? After several weeks, the 4th, 5th, and 6th grade classroom teachers began to see an improvement in behavior, motivation, and confidence as well. It was so successful that although our first year with the TinT program was only housed in one school, we grew it to five schools during year two, and it will be in 13 schools [in its third year].

Jackie and Marissa had a wholehearted vision for supporting students with challenging behavior that relied on love and respect rather than discipline and management. They took their new idea to their administrators and were given the green light to expand their program into additional grades across the district. We think this program's success is evidence enough to encourage you to take whatever heartfelt idea you have and put it into action.

Using the Jigsaw Strategy

Though there are many examples of cooperative learning that help build positive relationships and community among students, we want to go into detail about the Jigsaw Strategy because of its powerful history. It was used to defuse explosive racial tensions and significant challenging behaviors during school desegregation in Texas. In 1971, Austin's schools had recently been desegregated, and for the first time white, African American, and Latinx students were learning together in classes.

The fear and distrust between students due to decades of segregation exploded in an atmosphere of hostility and chaos. Physical fights erupted constantly, racial slurs were hurled, and teachers didn't know how to dispel these challenging behaviors. Austin's school superintendent brought in Dr. Eliot Aronson, a psychologist at the local university to see if he could observe and provide strategies to restore peace among the students in the city's schools. Dr. Aronson explained that his decision to create the cooperative Jigsaw Strategy was based on the following simple observation:

> It took only a few days of observation and interviews for us to see what was going on in these classrooms. We realized that we needed to shift the emphasis from a relentlessly competitive atmosphere to a more cooperative one. It was in this context that we invented the Jigsaw Strategy. (Aronson, 2000a, para 4)

Essentially, the Jigsaw Strategy requires students to work together in small groups in order to learn from one another. The small groups are purposefully grouped in heterogeneous ways, and the learning process is highly structured and facilitated by the teacher so individual student competition becomes incompatible with success. Students can only do well when they are cooperative in their behavior. Perhaps most important, each student, no matter their skill levels, language, or prior knowledge, should be placed in a position to bring the group a vital piece of knowledge that was not readily available without them.

Aronson and his team of graduate students taught the teachers how to utilize the Jigsaw Strategy (Aronson & Bridgeman, 1979). They then randomly introduced the Jigsaw Strategy to some classrooms, but not others, in order to study the outcomes. Aronson and his team found that after only eight weeks, there were significant differences between the classes that used the Jigsaw Strategy and the classes that did not. The findings showed that students in classes using the Jigsaw Strategy expressed less prejudice and negative stereotyping toward peers, were more self-confident, and reported liking school more than students who did not participate in the Jigsaw Strategy in class.

Students in classrooms using the Jigsaw Strategy were absent less often and showed greater academic improvement. Specifically, students who were identified as low-income scored significantly higher on exams than their low-income counterparts in classrooms not implementing the Jigsaw Strategy. Finally, fighting between demographic groups decreased and students learned to empathize more effectively with one another.

The Impact Community and Cooperation Makes

One of the most powerful stories that came from this research was about a student Aronson referred to as Carlos. Aronson described Carlos as shy and insecure in his new school. He spoke English well, but his new classmates were white, native English speakers, and in such a hostile climate, they were quick to call Carlos stupid when he spoke with a Spanish accent and stumbled over his words.

Carlos was part of an intervention classroom that was experimenting with the Jigsaw Strategy. In these new groups where students had to learn individual content and then come back to teach their group members what they had learned, the situation between Carlos and his peers changed. Once that they had to work together in order to do well, their negative behaviors (i.e., cutting Carlos down with cruel words) harmed each student's chance to do well in class. Aronson recalled what happened after only a few days using the Jigsaw Strategy with Carlos and his group:

> Carlos's groupmates gradually realized that they needed to change their tactics. It was no longer in their own best interest to rattle Carlos. They needed him to perform well in order to do well themselves. In effect, they had to put themselves in Carlos's shoes in order to find a way to ask questions that didn't undermine his performance.
>
> After a week or two, most of Carlos's groupmates developed into skillful interviewers, asking him relevant questions and helping him articulate clear answers. As Carlos succeeded, his groupmates began to see him in a more positive light. Moreover, Carlos saw himself in a new light, as a competent member of the class who could work with others from different ethnic groups. His self-esteem grew, and as it grew, his performance improved even more. In addition, Carlos began to see his groupmates as friendly and supportive. (Aronson, 2000a, paras. 8–9)

Ten years later, in 1982, Aronson received a letter in the mail from Carlos. During his undergraduate studies at the University of Texas, he had read Aronson's book *The Social Animal* (1972), which detailed his research with the Jigsaw Strategy in Austin schools. Carlos recognized himself in the book and remembered how he felt at school that year in 5th grade. In his letter to Aronson, he wrote,

> I remembered you when you first came to our classroom and how I was scared and how I hated school and how I was so stupid and didn't know anything. . . .

And most important, when we started to do work in jigsaw groups, I began to realize that I wasn't really that stupid. And the kids I thought were cruel and hostile became my friends. The teacher acted friendly and nice to me and I actually began to love school. I began to love to learn things, and now I'm about to go to Harvard Law School.

You must get a lot of letters like this, but I decided to write anyway because let me tell you something. My mother tells me that when I was born, I almost died. I was born at home and the cord was wrapped around my neck and the midwife gave me mouth to mouth and saved my life. If she were still alive, I would write to her, too, to tell her that I grew up smart and good and I'm going to law school. But she died a few years ago. I'm writing to you because, no less than her, you saved my life, too. (Aronson, 2000b, paras. 2–4)

If you want to read Carlos's full letter to Aronson or read more about the Jigsaw Strategy, you can find all this information on Aronson's website (www.jigsaw.org/history/carlos.html). But for now, we'd love you to pause and consider the life-changing work we do as educators when we build community and help students cultivate love and respect for one another.

Using Collaborative Research Projects

This type of formal cooperative learning is similar to the Jigsaw Strategy but often gets students to dive deeper into the work. Because they don't stop at the end of the lesson and continue as ongoing projects, these projects provide students with greater opportunities to take on different roles that highlight their individual strengths and engage them in a variety of diverse activities (e.g., writer, researcher, video creator, interviewer, digital mastermind, artist, choreographer).

Collaborative research projects often utilize trips to the school library or computer lab, but teaching about reliance and love for community should extend beyond the classroom. Fortunately, there are many ways to focus students on making an impact and connecting with the broader community. When we design or codesign a community-focused collaborative research project with our students, we instill the values of understanding community needs and the importance of approaching community members and leaders as experts.

Collaborative research projects that affect the community also provide students with an opportunity to view school and learning as something much greater than the four classroom walls they typically spend so much time within. Working in connection to the community generally requires students to address a wider variety of learning styles and strengths (e.g., visual, kinesthetic, auditory, musical, exploratory, analytical). This is key to help support those students who have challenging behavior largely because they may struggle in typical school settings with more traditional classwork. New ways to "do school" can allow them to shine, share their strengths and talents, and connect them in authentic and meaningful ways to their communities. A few collaborative research projects that have inspired us over the past few years include the following examples:

- Fourth grade students created a digital story to educate an audience (their 4th and 5th grade peers) about a current event (the 2018 midterm elections in the United States).
- High school students created and published a four-series podcast on the #BlackLivesMatter movement, and they interviewed members from the organized chapter in their hometown.
- Middle school students wrote and filmed a documentary film as a way to explore a looming community problem (the history of and future plans for a recently closed paper mill).
- Middle school students wrote, directed, and acted in a short play about mitosis and meiosis.
- Second and third grade students created an art installation and presented a historical and future examination about why their community needed more reliable public transportation.

We love collaborative research projects because they build connections between students and connect students to their communities. It's one more step in the direction of creating an inclusive culture in which students belong with and rely on one another and their community.

Inclusive Culture Comes from Everywhere

Creating an inclusive culture can begin in a multitude of places—leadership, faculty, staff, or with students themselves. Once the process of creating an inclusive culture is put into motion by someone—be it a 2nd grade teacher, a custodian, a parent, or even a superintendent—we know that the inclusive mindset and practices can then grow exponentially. When we work to reshape our schools to welcome a particular type of student—a student with challenging behavior, a student with a disability, or a multilingual language learner—what we find is that inclusion affects everybody in positive and often life-changing ways. It only takes one individual to set something inclusive in motion.

Perhaps as you read this, you are thinking, "How could I, one teacher, parent, or principal, inspire a movement toward a greater inclusive culture in my school?" This is a common feeling. We've felt it ourselves, and we hear about it at every level. We've met parents who feel they can't make a difference unless they're on the school board. We've met teachers who feel they can't make a difference because there aren't enough resources, support, or appropriate structures provided by leadership. We've met principals, directors of special education, and directors of curriculum and instruction who feel they can't make a difference because it's not a priority for the superintendent. We've met superintendents who feel they can't make a difference because they are beholden to the school board, parents, or financial issues.

The gift we want to give you today, right now, is the gift of agency. You—parent, teacher, principal, counselor, superintendent, or whatever your title may be—have the agency to make a difference in the inclusive culture in your school, in both small and big ways. So say it with us now: "I have the agency to make an inclusive difference."

What we know is that when you simply begin, people will take notice of your work. They might join you in the conversation about inclusion, how to do it, and for whom. As you continue on your journey, making small or big inclusive shifts, others in your school community will begin to see the positive impact it has had on your students and you. Then they'll want to get involved. Soon, more individuals will join you and more robust changes can occur. In fact, when many people begin to believe in their individual agency and when they approach inclusive work from a place of love and empowerment, we begin to see real, meaningful, inclusive culture develop in schools.

In the next section, we want to share a few examples of individuals we know who have taken the first steps toward meaningful inclusive culture change, both big and small, in their schools and districts.

Dr. Jenna Inspires Change

Dr. Jenna is the assistant superintendent for a large suburban district in Pennsylvania. She worked there for many years, holding different roles, including special education supervisor at the local high school and director of special education and student services. Jenna is a wildly accomplished educator who describes her work as a calling and a passion. We think she is a magnificent example of the hope and change one person can inspire.

Over the years, she has been influential in creating greater inclusive culture and structures in her district. Jenna began at the high school, creating coteaching teams to support diverse students in general education classes. Later, as the director of special education, she was the driving force behind the implementation of the district's inclusion facilitator model, in which special education teachers are given the freedom to focus solely on providing inclusive support to students and teachers. When funding became an issue, Jenna didn't let it slow her down. She applied for and received a national innovation grant to support the work of inclusion. Today, her district is one of the most inclusive districts in the state of Pennsylvania with more than 32 inclusion facilitators working in the district. Every day, administrators, teachers, parents, and students collaborate to implement the ongoing work of inclusion for all.

Johanna Makes Inclusive Waves

When we first heard about Johanna, she was preparing to include Nina, a 3rd grade student with complex support needs, in her general education class for the first time in her school's history. Nina was a student who had been described by her previous school team as challenging. She was labeled as having an intellectual disability, communication and social delays, and very challenging behavior during transitions and activities that were difficult for her.

Johanna met Nina, reviewed her Individual Education Program (IEP) with the special education teacher, and met with Nina's mother, who shared a beautiful positive profile of her daughter (think back to Chapter 1 and the creation of a holistic student profile that highlighted strengths, interests, and strategies that work). She decided that in order to include Nina in an authentic and meaningful way, she would shake things up and create activity stations and focus on small-group instruction. The learning stations and small-group work provided Johanna with opportunities to give Nina the accommodations and modifications she needed while also, she realized, benefitting all of her students.

For example, at that time, Nina was unable to decode, and this often made her behavior challenging during reading activities. Johanna made sure she set up reading buddies and a reading station to support Nina. She also rotated reading buddies so Nina worked with many of her peers, and she purposefully facilitated connections between the buddies to build a culture of support and friendship. For example, she would say, "Nina and Danny, both of you love stories about animals. Would you like to read this book about wolves together?" Johanna also made sure there were plenty of other opportunities for peers to work closely with Nina on academic tasks and social activities, such as math buddy checks, in which one student would check answers to math problems with a calculator while Nina solved the same problems using manipulatives.

Nina had difficulty with transitions and was considered a "flight risk," so she always had a paraprofessional hold her hand while moving through the school building. But Johanna and the special education teacher decided that instead of this assumption, they would home in on her strengths and interests. They said, "Let's get her excited about transitioning through the building and see if she no longer wants to run away." They created a job for her—librarian's helper—in which she moved through the school with a cart, collecting books from classrooms and returning them to the library. The job drew on her strengths. She was sociable, loved stories, and liked to be a leader, and it also addressed her challenging behaviors around transitions in the building. Ultimately, she was able to complete her daily job with great success. Overall, Johanna found Nina's transitions improved dramatically and by mid-year, she was volunteering to lead the class line from the classroom to lunch or specials.

Johanna's thoughtful inclusion of Nina had a significant positive effect on other students, too. In the beginning of the year, John could barely read. When Johanna started the peer prereading strategy, John realized that Nina loved listening to stories. As her reading buddy, he began reading her simple picture books. She listened and learned while John's confidence and reading fluency grew. By the end of the year, he was reading chapter books to her. Nina's friend Elias struggled with focus and attention, but when he worked with Nina, he was patient, calm, and loving. "What I have come to realize," Elias's mom wrote to Johanna, "is that having Nina in class has helped Elias in more ways than I could have imagined. It has taught him so much and he truly loves her."

Johanna's efforts to create a positive inclusive culture made great waves in her district. The administration took note of the benefits of Nina's inclusion and Johanna's heartfelt, hard work. The following year, the district began focusing efforts on increasing its inclusive programming for all students with disabilities in two more elementary schools. The eventual goal is to create more inclusion at all levels in the district—elementary, middle, and high school.

Working Together to Create Access and Inclusive Culture

At a high school in a large suburban district in the Northeast, students were the inspiration for creating an inclusive culture that spanned the district. It began with Isabella, a middle school student who loves learning but has quadriplegia and is therefore unable to communicate her thoughts in a verbal way. For most of Isabella's school career, she used assistive technology we might consider "low tech." She used her eyes to gaze and choose multiple choice questions offered by educators and paraeducators in order to participate in her general education classes. But in 7th grade, it became clear that Isabella's multiple-choice options and assistive tech weren't helping her communicate and participate to her full potential. She needed a high-tech device to provide her with improved access both in and out of class. Her teachers envisioned an eye-gaze device that connected to Isabella's laptop and would interface with many of the computer programs her classes used while also providing increased access to social phrases so she could connect naturally and more often with peers.

However, eye-gaze devices are expensive. Therefore, her teachers hatched an idea and asked the district's high school technology and engineering department for help. The department chair shared the challenge with his students, who, after learning about Isabella's access issues, were immediately invested in building her an inexpensive eye-gaze device. "She's going to be [in high school] in a few years," one student said. "We need to figure this out now." And, just like that, Project Hawk-Eye was born.

The students worked before and after school to build Isabella's eye-gaze technology. They problem solved roadblocks without complaining because they knew Isabella's access to learning and communication was at stake. When the circuit board they purchased didn't work, they built a new one rather than going over budget. When they were nearly done, they realized the device would be too heavy for Isabella to wear. They started over, creating new, lighter parts on a 3D printer. These high schoolers became passionate about a critical social justice issue within their own school community. They became invested in Isabella's success and were able to see how their ideas and learning could create a more inclusive solution for her. Isabella, in turn, felt supported, valued, and included by her peers, who talked excitedly to her about the device and their hopes for it to help her. The enthusiasm and energy around inclusion and supporting one another spread throughout the school community. The chair of the high school technology and engineering department seemed to capture the experience perfectly: "Our students now understand that, yes, we *can* change the world."

Developing Habits of Mind

An inclusive culture change can start with you. Your actions can help your classroom, school, and district focus on belonging and access for all students, including those with challenging behaviors. To embark on the courageous journey of change, it is helpful to focus on developing three habits of mind: persistence, strength, and patience.

- We must persist even when the work is difficult.
- We must have the strength to love our students and lean into our values even when there is resistance.
- We must have the patience to continue the work, even when we don't see immediate results.

 **Tiny To-Do List**

❏ Write down and begin implementing your ideas for building relationships with students through daily actions.
❏ Reflect on which formal and informal strategies you want to try to cultivate love and reliance in your class and school community.
❏ Write down your own habits of mind that will help you commit to creating an inclusive culture even when the going gets tough.

Teaching Gratitude, Kindness, and Compassion

In this chapter, we focus on how you can teach students important social and emotional skills such as kindness, compassion, gratitude, and trust. We provide strategies, ideas, and resources you can use daily in your classrooms or throughout your entire school. We also address the research about these practices both in and out of schools and how implementation in your classroom connects to building kinder, more compassionate school communities while also minimizing challenging behavior.

Understanding Social-Emotional Learning

Social-emotional learning (SEL) is the process through which students learn to understand and manage emotions; set and achieve positive goals; feel and show empathy, kindness, and compassion for themselves and others; establish and maintain positive relationships; and make responsible decisions. SEL is a critical aspect of emotional intelligence (EQ) and is an important predictor of life success and happiness. There is exciting research about how we can teach students social and emotional skills that will build resilience, gratitude, self-compassion, and kindness to others (Durlak, Weissberg, Dymnicki, Taylor, & Schellinger, 2011). An entire center at the University of Wisconsin–Madison has dedicated significant time and resources to understanding the specific activities teachers can use to support students' well-being.

Many teachers we know have found that learning more about SEL has helped reduce the challenging behavior in their classrooms, and it has helped them understand how important it is to focus on their own health and well-being. Nancy, an inclusive 5th grade teacher, told Kate that she began sharing her authentic knowledge about health and well-being with her students because she was practicing self-care and self-compassion with herself. She was able to connect more deeply with her students who had challenging behavior and who came to school unregulated, anxious, and angry. She explains, "When *I* talked about being stressed and how I practiced keeping my focus on aspects of my own happiness, students found they could reflect upon their own practices. Then I started setting aside time during our Monday morning meetings to talk about how we spent our time focused on our own happiness and well-being over the weekend and how we could keep a focus on that during our school week, too" (personal communication, June 15, 2019).

Nancy found that all her students benefited from these conversations during the Monday morning meeting, learning specific practices to help them improve their own well-being and having the opportunity to engage in this work meaningfully during their school day. Nancy was surprised, however, to learn that these practices had the most profound impact on her most anxious and angry students.

Nancy and other teachers like her are successfully tapping into the research-based strategies and benefits of social and emotional learning. However, before we move on to the research and strategies about teaching students self-compassion, gratitude, and kindness, we'd love you to take the time to pause, reflect, and write about the following concepts:

- How would you benefit from exploring practices of self-compassion, gratitude, and kindness?
- In what ways do you hope exploring self-compassion, gratitude, and kindness with yourself and your students will affect your classroom?

Teaching Self-Compassion

We often talk about self-esteem and its importance for student success and happiness. Although self-esteem is certainly useful, Dr. Kristin Neff, a psychologist who studies compassion, has shown that self-compassion is actually a much more powerful socioemotional tool if we want to improve our happiness and success.

In her extensive research, Neff (2003) has identified three key elements of self-compassion on which we'll focus here: kindness, a common humanity, and mindfulness. When practiced together, these three concepts interact to create a truly self-compassionate frame of mind that helps us significantly when we are faced with failures, mistakes, issues of confidence, and any mental, emotional, or physical pain. Using this information to support our students with challenging behavior can be a key element to unlocking their potential to achieve happiness and success in our classrooms and beyond, despite the external forces with which they might be barraged on a daily basis.

Teaching Kids to Talk to Themselves with Self-Kindness

It is all too easy for students to talk to themselves unkindly. This is because as humans, we are so often our own worst critics. Research shows that most people are kinder to others than they are to themselves (Neff, 2003). When our students, particularly those who are communicating a great need to us through challenging behavior, continue to use negative and unkind talk with themselves, they can internalize false ideas about who they are and what they can become or achieve. In order to break this negative cycle, we must provide them with language, strategies, and many opportunities to practice how to be supportive and understanding toward themselves, particularly when they are suffering, in pain, feeling stressed, angry, or out of control. By facilitating this social-emotional learning for them, we can effectively help students soothe and nurture themselves using gentler and encouraging self-talk.

Psychologists explain that when we use kind, encouraging language with ourselves during moments of difficulty, we become emotionally moved by our own feelings of distress (Neff & Germer, 2017). When this happens, warm and kind feelings can emerge. Those same feelings might come up when we are helping others with kindness when they are in distress. We can then use those same warm feelings to reduce our own pain and discomfort. In this way, we can teach students to validate their feelings and emotions rather than instantly try to fix them.

Students can then soothe and comfort themselves when they need it and create new stories about who they are and what they can become.

The following activities are useful for teaching students gentle and encouraging self-talk, either on their own or in a scaffolded way:

- For primary classrooms, read *Listening with My Heart* by Gabi Garcia (2017) with the class and talk about how the main character, Esperanza, shows compassion to others but not to herself. Brainstorm ways she could have talked kindlier and with more compassion to herself during moments of frustration.

- For all ages, use a class meeting or connection circle to introduce compassion and self-compassion. Together, brainstorm a list of experiences you've all had when something doesn't go right (e.g., failing a test; getting in a fight with a parent, friend, or teacher; losing a game). Then brainstorm some of the common responses you tell yourself when these not-so-great experiences happen. Often, ideas such as "I'm so dumb," "I don't know how to ___," or "I'm no good at ___" emerge.

- Finally, ask the class to brainstorm what they might tell their friends when they are struggling with these same experiences or what they'd like to hear from a friend. After this activity, you might turn their ideas into a chart you can then provide to students as a starting place for teaching concepts of health, happiness, and well-being (see Figure 5.1).

Figure 5.1: Creating Kinder and More Encouraging Self-Talk

Harmful Self-Talk	Kind and Encouraging Self-Talk
• I'm so stupid. • I'll never have any friends. • There's no way I'll pass this test. • No one cares about me or how I feel.	• This is really hard for me right now. • I feel lonely right now. • I'm feeling anxious. I can study hard and ask my teacher and friends for help. • I deserve to be cared about and understood.

Encouraging a Common Humanity: Teaching Kids They Are Not Alone

We all get it wrong sometimes—because we are human! But unlearning the myths of perfection in order to embrace the concept of being perfectly imperfect can take years or even decades. As sociologist Dr. Brené Brown explains in her book *The Gifts of Imperfection* (2010), to live wholeheartedly with compassion, kindness, and gratitude, we must begin by

> Cultivating the courage, compassion, and connection to wake up in the morning and think, "No matter what gets done and how much is left undone, I am enough." It's going to bed at night thinking, "Yes, I am imperfect and vulnerable and sometimes afraid, but that doesn't change the truth that I am also brave and worthy of love and belonging." (p. 1)

We want to help our students understand that even if they lose the game, hurt a friend's feelings, or make a mistake in a group project, they are still worthy of love and belonging. A way to help students understand that it is OK to have disappointments, both in themselves or their circumstances, is to help them see that they are not alone in these feelings and experiences. This explicit work is useful to ensure students don't feel isolated in their struggles and failures. When we help students see themselves as people who will sometimes fail and make mistakes, we can have what Neff and Dahm (2014) describe as the following broader perspective: "By remembering the shared human experience, we feel less isolated when we are in pain."

We can help students cultivate a mindset that is more deeply connected to others and their experiences while also boosting self-compassion in themselves.

Practicing Mindfulness: Teaching Kids the Art of Being in the Moment

Mindfulness can help us face the present moment without judgment for ourselves or others, and without avoiding or repressing our emotions or ideas. This can be very difficult because it means we must be willing to sit with painful thoughts and emotions in order to approach ourselves with self-compassion and kindness. It is easy for us and our students to get lost in their distress or anger or to move so quickly into solving the issue at hand that we do not pause to consider the difficulty, anger, or sadness the issue causes. When we teach students to be mindful of their feelings, we can help them understand that they aren't defined by their emotions and feelings. We can help students recognize that their thoughts and feelings do not get to decide who they are or who they will be.

Mrs. Smith, an elementary school teacher we know, connected with JusTme, a hip-hop and mindfulness instructor out of Oakland, California, to use his Mindful Sits with her students. Known offstage as Timothy Earl Scott Jr, his sits are seven-minute exercises that students can use to regroup and ready themselves for afternoon lessons (JusTme, 2020). Mrs. Smith believes the sits get students in a loving and caring mindset that helps them focus on creating positive self-affirmations that help them make it through even the busiest, most challenging days. She was fascinated because she found that her students who had the most difficulty sitting still and "doing school"—those who behaved in expected ways— really loved the sits. She found that once they became pros at the Mindful Sits, she could send them to help teach younger students in school, and it helped improve their behaviors throughout the day.

Using Writing Practices to Teach Self-Compassion

For primary or secondary classrooms, you can have students write about a difficult time in their lives when they felt not good enough, disappointed in themselves, or frustrated when things didn't go as they had planned or hoped. Then ask them to write ways they could have talked to and treated themselves kindly and gently. We recommend providing an example from your own life.

Students can also practice writing in daily or weekly journals in which they write a kind and compassionate letter to themselves. Several years ago, researchers conducted an experiment in which some individuals were asked to write a self-compassionate letter to themselves every day for seven days, while others were asked to write about childhood memories every day for seven days (Shapira & Mongrain, 2010). The researchers found that those who wrote self-compassionate letters reported increased happiness as opposed to the group that wrote only about memories. Perhaps the most intriguing finding to us is that the group that wrote self-compassionate letters to themselves also reported that their increased happiness levels persisted one, three, and six months after the study. With this type of research in support, we recommend helping students write self-compassionate letters to themselves.

Helping Students Strengthen Their Inner Nurturer

Our students begin developing their own inner nurturer through experiences of nurturing from parents, guardians, older children, and, of course, teachers. We can help students strengthen their inner nurturers, particularly for those who may have experienced less nurturing and more criticism and trauma in their lives. We can support them by helping them create a "caring committee" or "circle of support" made up of individuals who represent kindness, compassion, and wisdom for them.

For example, Kate's caring committee is composed of her husband, her parents, several close friends, and her late grandfather. When she's feeling in need of additional nurturing, she turns to fictional characters such as Marmee March, the mother in Louisa May Alcott's *Little Women* who provides her daughters with incredible support and wisdom throughout the book, or Elle Woods from *Legally Blonde,* with her peppy, positive, can-do spirit. We recommend asking your students to build their own caring committees that are made up of real and fictional characters who can guide them through difficult times with kindness, compassion, and wisdom.

Teaching Gratitude

Gratitude can be defined in many ways. We know we've asked you to consider gratitude when we wrote about care and love for yourself in Chapter 3, but for our purposes here, we want to discuss a particular definition from Dr. Kerry Howells (2019). Howells is a researcher who studies the unique connections between gratitude and education, and she explains that gratitude is "the action of giving back out of acknowledgment for what we have received, in ways that are not necessarily reciprocal" (p. 181). You'll notice that she uses the word *action* in this definition because in her research, she has learned that it is not until we express gratitude through action that it becomes authentic and beneficial for us.

It is indeed certainly useful to mentally practice your gratitude; however, it is only when you turn that into an action can it turn into a practice that really benefits you and others. For example, you can greet your students by telling them how grateful you are for them to be in school today.

The Benefits of Gratitude for Our Students

Practicing gratitude and the many other positive emotions that go hand in hand with the practice provides us with significant benefit. Gratitude improves our connection with others; helps us recover from trauma, loss, and negative experiences; and improves our physical health by strengthening our immune system and protecting our cardiovascular system. Gratitude can also help us widen our perspective, valuing not only what is good in the present moment but also the opportunities for our future.

When teachers practice gratitude, the positive benefits get even more specific. Teachers who engage in a regular practice of gratitude in their classrooms report that they give greater priority to relationships with students (rather than tasks), develop greater collegiality with faculty, feel calmer, have a greater overall sense of well-being, and are more engaged with their students.

Positive psychologist Dr. Philip Watkins (2015), who studies happiness and gratitude, found that because gratitude works similarly to a muscle, we must flex it in order to build its strength. The physical act of writing down our gratitude can help us strengthen our gratitude practice. Watkins also found that people who have the most difficult time finding gratitude actually benefit the most from flexing their gratitude muscles and writing them down. This is powerful news for students and adults who might feel they have little to be grateful for due to difficult life experiences.

In a study that focused specifically on middle school students, Jeffrey Froh (Froh, Miller, & Snyder, 2007) had a small group of students practice gratitude every day by writing down five things they were grateful for in a gratitude journal. He found that students who were engaged in this practice reported greater optimism, improved satisfaction with their lives, and decreased negative feelings when compared to their peers who were not engaged in the daily gratitude practice.

Celebrating Small, Beautiful Moments

We know that happiness can be cultivated just by thinking about, remembering, and sharing the details of a particularly delightful moment. When students engage in this purposeful work, they raise their feelings of happiness and reexperience it in their body. This not only helps them feel happier in the moment and throughout their day but also helps them stay more in tune with positive experiences and helps recenter them when they feel they are going off course. This practice can help students feel more positive about their school day and their lives and help them build the skills to face difficulties with calmness and an understanding that things will get better. What follows are a few examples we love that can help your students in this practice:

- **Quick Jot:** At the end of the day, have students close their eyes and think of a positive moment. It can be a small moment or a big one. Then have them write about that experience. Finally, invite them to consider and feel each detail in the experience.

- **Turn and Celebrate:** We love the idea of ending each class period by having students stop, find a partner, and share one happy moment from that class or day. For students who may not want to talk or are nonverbal, you can invite them to write about or share pictures about what made them happy during the day. When they are done sharing, encourage them to give one another a high five or a fist bump.

- **Blog It:** Create a blog post at the end of the class period or week where each student shares or writes one great moment from the day or week. If blogging isn't your thing, create a Twitter or Instagram account that students can tag with their tiny beautiful moments. It can be as simple as the following example: "@SHS6periodELA: Today I used the Pythagorean theorem correctly! #tinymoments." Whether it's a blog or a social media feed, by the end of the school year, your class will have collected thousands of small, beautiful moments they can read, remember, and enjoy.

- **Share the News:** Cultivate happiness by creating a Daily Happenings newsletter during down time at the end of the week. Ask each student to share something about one of their best moments. You, a paraprofessional, or a student can type the moments up for the newsletter and then send it home. Parents at the secondary level are not often as involved in their child's schooling, and parents have reported that they love learning about the day through this newsletter.

- **Share a Note:** One teacher we know shared with us that he writes tiny notes or draws simple images on sticky notes or small index cards a few times a week. Each note is filled with specific praise and gratitude for a particular student. For example, he might write, "I love how you helped Aidan during lab today" or "Your comment about Mercutio's anger was so insightful today." He then shares these messages of love at random points throughout the day, and he asks students to share the note with friends, parents, or other supporters.

• **Gratitude Showers:** Paige, an ELA teacher whom Kate knows and admires, decided to boost the mood of her entire middle school after learning about the research behind the practice of gratitude. She created what she called "gratitude showers" for the school community. To begin, she engaged her classes in a weeklong project focused on two 7th grade writing standards (CCSS.ELA-LITERACY.WHST.6-8.4 and CCSS.ELA-LITERACY.WHST.6-8.6).

She had students choose various videos and articles to read and watch regarding the practice and impact of gratitude. She engaged students in a dialogue about their findings and then asked students to create a list of people and things they were grateful for in the school community. She taught them how to plan and write a variety of informal and formal thank-you notes. Students then took on the task of writing the notes and worked together as peer reviewers to revise and edit their work.

Paige then had students vote to deliver their messages of gratitude in fun and varied ways. Several students created video messages that were delivered over email or posted to the school's website, along with relevant links to articles about the practice and benefits of gratitude. Another set of students put sticky notes on student lockers before the start of the school day. Afterward, they conducted follow-up interviews with involved students (both the receiver and giver) to find out how the messages affected them and then documented their findings on the classroom blog.

• **Interdisciplinary Gratitude:** Draw on the creative and interdisciplinary work of your colleagues to teach students the art *and* science of being grateful. One school team we know engaged students in a two-week interdisciplinary unit connecting health, art, and science in order to study both the art and science of gratitude. Students' culminating projects were shared with the entire school community on a Gratitude Night and included research studies about the brain and gratitude, a photography series, and an experiential gratitude art installation.

Teaching Kindness and Compassion for Others

Deep social connections are a serious predictor of happiness and well-being. So if we are creating classrooms from a place of love, we must help our students learn and practice kindness and compassion with one another. This is particularly important when we consider the tense, uncomfortable dynamics that can build between peers and a student who is displaying challenging behavior. The last thing we want is for our students who are struggling most to feel isolated from their peers and from kind and compassionate connections.

Setting the Intention of Kindness

Whether students are learning how to be kind or how to solve mathematical equations, success in learning is deeply connected to a person's intentions. When we participate in activities for which we have created clear intentions, we release dopamine, feel pleasure, and experience increased focus, memory, and motivation. But so often, the intentions our students set for themselves are connected only to academic success and achievement.

In fact, a study of 10,000 middle and high school kids showed that 62 percent of kids believe their teachers consider academic achievement to be more important than kindness or caring for others (Grant, 2014). In order to change our students' perspectives, we must set our own intention of teaching and valuing kindness. We can then begin to put kindness on display and into action in our classrooms and schools, particularly for those students who are struggling most. We must show our students that we carve out time and energy for teaching kindness because we believe in its importance and its value in our lives and theirs.

Once we set those initial intentions, we can also explore the links between kindness and academic achievement with our students. We can explain that when kids practice kindness and empathy, they have increased academic success (Jones & Bouffard, 2012). As our students get older, we can help them understand that the same applies to their post-school lives. People who are kind and collaborative in the workplace and generous with their time and ideas are more likely to have better professional outcomes than their colleagues who focus only on professional achievement and advancement (Grant, 2014).

Practices for Teaching Kindness and Compassion for Others

Once you set this intention with yourself and your students, you can begin implementing specific practices for teaching kindness and compassion. Here are a few practices we love:

- **Habits of Kind Kids:** Have your class research the habits of people who practice kindness, compassion, and generosity. Students can use this research to create all sorts of creative products to share about the "habits of kind kids." In fact, at a middle school in Nashville, kindness was a schoolwide focus set by the principal. During the first quarter of school, students from all the 6th grade communities worked on habits of kind kids research projects. The project culminated with The Habits of Kind Kids Event, in which the school's students, teachers, and families were invited to learn about the 6th grade projects. Students put on a short play, read poetry, and presented their research. They ended the night with a short film they had created featuring the entire 6th grade implementing the kind habits around school.

- **Kindness Centers:** Set up a kindness center in your classroom or school where students can go to read, discuss books, watch videos, and research about kindness and compassion. An elementary school teacher we know set up a kindness center in her room and made it an integral part of her daily center work rotations. She often used the center as a place to connect more deeply to concepts and skills around celebrating inclusion and friendship. This included skills such as how to be patient with friends, how to encourage and include others in activities, and how to celebrate our differences.

- **Kindness Challenge:** Students can create a kindness challenge and commit to completing kind acts for a week, a month, or an entire quarter or semester. Students can document their kind acts and compile them at the end of the challenge to create a blog or publish them in a book.

Kate did a version of the last example—which she called the 21 Days of Kindness Challenge—with a freshman seminar class at the University of Maine, Farmington (UMF) in order to help them fulfill a project centered around an essential question they had posed: "How do we create kinder and more inclusive campus communities?" The students created a social media campaign using Twitter,

Facebook, Instagram, Snapchat, and the university's website to spread the news about the challenge.

For 21 days, students recorded and documented themselves completing kind acts and posted them to social media all while encouraging other students and faculty to take up the kindness challenge themselves. The results were exciting. Students left kind notes for strangers, professors, and friends on cars, dorm doors, and office doors. They hung inspiring quotes in hallways, gave passersby flowers, shoveled snow for a neighbor, cooked dinner for friends, and bought coffee for students studying in the library.

Kate's students found that not only did they feel better about themselves after being kind and spreading gratitude and kindness, but they felt more successful. They could see the effect they had on other students and faculty who began implementing their own acts of kindness. They were also sharing their actions on social media using the hashtag #umfkindness. An upperclassman who was handed a flower was encouraged to join the challenge and later shared, "I think it is so awesome that students are doing something like this to create a kinder culture on campus. It is really needed, and the flower and kind words just absolutely brightened my day!"

 **Tiny To-Do List**

- ❑ Use your journal to complete the reflection exercise at the beginning of this chapter.
- ❑ Write down ways you can help your students understand that you value kindness and compassion in your classroom.
- ❑ Challenge yourself to implement one of the practices in this chapter with your students.

Exploring Acceptance, Belonging, and Community:
Heartfelt Problem Solving

In this chapter, we share a collaborative problem-solving approach to use with students. We ask educators to reflect on their responses to student behavior and invest in building relationships—instead of barriers—with students. We discuss practices that support educators to do this work, including giving students ownership over the process, encouraging peers to work together to develop new ideas and mediate existing problems (a practice that aligns well with restorative practices), and leading colleagues to help create success plans for students.

Moving from Control to Love

In order to use a collaborative, heartfelt approach to creating inclusive and student-centered learning environments, we first must let go of the idea that control and compliance are best for our students and for us. This can be hard, especially when we have increasingly diverse behavioral needs and large class sizes. Nevertheless, if we are to reach our students despite these very real issues, we must take on the following:

- Believe that all our students are capable and motivated to learn academically, emotionally, and socially.
- Respect our students by allowing them to have ownership in the process of this learning and decision making.
- Trust that our students, like us, are committed to building and sustaining a caring classroom community.
- Understand that everyone has less-than-good days, and that on those days, we need more love, trust, and caring—not less.

Removing Quick Fixes: There Are No Shortcuts Here

We understand why educators and parents want a quick fix to behavioral issues. It is painful to watch a student struggle. It can be heartbreaking to be with students when they are out of control. It can be beyond frustrating to try to keep a classroom of students moving in a single direction when one or a few students are taking the entire lesson off track. It can also be difficult when it seems the behavior of a few is completely changing the feelings of the community or of everyone's security. We understand the desperation educators feel in this situation and therefore understand the appeal of quick fixes. We wish we could simply say, "Just do these simple things and your student's behavior will be back on track." Unfortunately, in most cases, if you really want to fix behavior, it requires a long-term commitment to providing consistency, love, and trust.

Moving from Timeouts to Trust

Imagine you are angry, frustrated, sad, scared, or confused. When these emotions occur, many of us behave in similar ways. We yell, stomp out of the room, cry, or curl up into a tiny ball on the floor or couch. Over the years, we have asked thousands of educators what they need to center or calm themselves when these emotions and behaviors surface in their own lives. The answers are often as simple as listening to music, receiving a hug, or having someone to talk to (who is willing to listen).

Now consider the many common school responses to students who are angry, frustrated, sad, or scared and who express these emotions by yelling, stomping out of the room, crying, or curling up in a ball under their desk. If your school is like the thousands of schools we've visited over the years, you might have responded with timeouts, a visit to the principal's office, or detention. Timeouts, punishments, and exclusionary practices are the all-too-common responses to challenging behavior. More troubling still, students with disabilities and students of color are at a far greater risk of these punishments and school exclusion practices than their white and nondisabled counterparts (U.S. Office for Civil Rights, 2016).

Instead of reacting in a way that we ourselves would not respond well to, we must shift our responses to a new approach, complete with empathy, understanding, and trust. We must trust that students, like us, need time, space, hugs, and someone to listen to them when they are feeling angry or hurt. They do *not* need to be physically removed, excluded from recess, or put into a room alone to calm down or think about their actions.

Think about this. What if we offered you a thousand dollars to go and tell as many people as you can to buy this book? It might increase our chances of getting more positive reviews on Amazon, Facebook, and Twitter. Therefore, you might say our incentive was effective in getting the desired behavior. However, when it comes to educating children, too many people believe that rewards and punishment work. In response, Alfie Kohn (1999) introduced two radically important questions countering this belief: "Work to do what? At what cost?"

Starting with the End in Mind

To really consider these questions, we must start with the end in mind. We must ask ourselves, "What is the purpose of education? What do we hope to achieve?" We have asked literally thousands of teachers these exact questions. Although their answers vary, there are several themes that have emerged from their answers.

What is the end goal in education? Many teachers have noted that they want to help develop students who are self-reliant, kind, responsible, socially skilled, caring, capable of surviving and succeeding in life, critical thinkers, confident, understanding of their own worth, open to new ideas, creative, courageous, resilient, and happy. Let's imagine you can agree to all or most of these goals.

Now go back up to that list and consider your daily practices and ask yourself, "Do our practices serve our larger goals? Do our rewards and punishments help us reach our end goals? Do rewards and punishments make students self-reliant or help them become kind, responsible, and socially skilled?" After really examining these questions, we find that rewards and punishments are, as Alfie Kohn explained in *Punished by Rewards* (1999), "worthless at best and destructive at worst" for helping students develop these values and skills (p. 230).

Do they work? Rewards and punishments might work to buy us temporary compliance or obedience, but they don't work for long-term growth or skill development. The downside is that when the punishment or reward is removed, the student loses motivation to continue the positive behavior.

At what cost? The costs of rewards and punishments have been long studied and well documented. They range from decreased motivation to trauma. When you go back to the scenario we presented about selling this book, the cost of getting these "good reviews" would be thousands of dollars, which is quite a steep cost to us. The cost of using rewards and punishments in schools can include something of much more value to students: the loss of self-esteem, intrinsic motivation, their ability to self-regulate, and self-direction. This can actually result in an increase in selfish and transactional thinking (e.g., "What will I get if I do that for you?").

Developing Heartfelt Problem Solving

After you have experienced extreme behavior that you know needs attention and support, you must then sit with the student to problem solve. Our traditional ways of supporting a student with challenging behavior include gathering a group of educators and administrators around a table, looking at data regarding antecedents that might cause the behavior, and determining strategies to prevent the behavior (along with consequences for the behavior if it occurs again). However, these strategies often fail because the student is not at the table working on solutions.

Why Collaborate? Understanding *Doing To* Versus *Doing With*

Traditional classroom management practices often focus on compliance and control of our students, whereas authentic collaboration with our students puts the emphasis on building student self-awareness and self-determination, responsibility, and empathy.

When we use traditional behavior management practices, such as rewards, consequences, teacher-created rules, and disciplinary procedures, we demonstrate a lack of trust in our students. This also decreases student trust in us. Although we may put an emphasis on rewards (e.g., good behavior points earn a class pizza party) rather than consequences (e.g., phone calls home, detentions, suspensions for bad behavior), we are still only attempting to control student behavior.

When we collaborate with students to set intentions about the classroom community and learning, we are asking them to use their own ideas and think critically about what authentic learning environments can and should be. We are allowing students to take risks, make mistakes, build and repair relationships, and—ultimately—take responsibility of their actions, both individually and collectively.

Empowering Students as Problem Solvers

When we work with our students instead of attempting to manage their behavior, we begin to position students as problem solvers. This helps them better understand themselves and their own needs, while also building more confident, creative, and empathetic decision makers.

We must begin by asking students what they need to be successful in certain situations. Then we must provide students with the space and time to brainstorm solutions to problems. Most important, we must allow them to implement their ideas and reflect on them.

Reinforcing Heartfelt Problem Solving: Acceptance, Belonging, and Community

Consequences have been a deeply held practice in behaviorism. The thinking behind it is that every behavior has a clear trigger (antecedent) and then the student gets something from that behavior (consequence). For example, Jenna continuously disrupts class during independent writing time by telling inappropriate jokes to peers. The teacher might assume that Jenna is seeking attention from her peers and teacher because she is trying to avoid the writing task.

Though this might be true, it is important to recognize that behavior is often too complex to always have a single, direct trigger. Therefore, heartfelt problem solving is a very different approach. First and foremost, it involves the student. It also considers the environment, context, rules, policies, teachers, and peers as part of the situation and the solution. When we use this broad view to address the problem, we ask more complex questions and approach solutions with greater creativity and depth. We use the following four steps to help our students move toward heartfelt problem solving:

Step 1: Discovering Strengths

Step 2: Discovering Challenges

Step 3: Dreaming and Designing for Increased Belonging

Step 4: Creating a Success Plan

Step 1: Discovering Strengths

We begin by using the following questions to focus only on positive aspects (do not discuss negative aspects at this point):

- What is currently working well?
- What is working well in the environment?
- What success exists already?
- Where are you feeling happiness or joy in your life?
- What are your strengths and talents?

Step 2: Discovering Challenges

In this step, we focus on challenges and model the following language to students: "I notice that . . ." For example, we might say, "I notice that reading time is not working well." You can also use the feelings chart in Figure 6.1 to help students who may have difficulty recognizing or expressing their feelings. Use the following questions to begin discussing challenges with your students:

- What is not working well?
- What challenges are you facing?
- What environmental factors are important?
- Where are you experiencing struggle? Can you be specific?
- Where are you feeling sad, frustrated, lonely, or hurt?
- Can you write for me how you are feeling?
- Can you draw for me how you are feeling?
- Can you point to how you are feeling?

After Step 2, we listen and study the big picture. We make educated guesses if the student has not been able to provide us with the understanding we may need. We then use the following steps to make sure we address all aspects of the situation:

- Consider the student holistically (i.e., strengths, skills, needs, family, friendships, history).
- Consider the policies and expectations we are attempting to enforce.
- Consider the supports we are providing.
- Consider the environment.
- Consider the teachers who are involved in the situation.
- Consider the student's peers.

Figure 6.1: Feelings Vocabulary Chart

Step 3: Dreaming and Designing for Increased Belonging

How can we dream and design ways to increase the student's belonging and connection at school while decreasing the difficult issue/behavior? Ask yourself, "What can I do to help?" and then use the following questions with your students:

- What kinds of support do you need?
- How can we take your successes to the next level?
- How do we continue to improve upon these strengths?
- How do we address these challenges?
- What can we do within the environment to make this better for you?
- Is there a friend who could support you with this?
- How could things feel better for all of us?

Step 4: Creating a Success Plan

You can begin this step by asking yourself, "How can we design a success plan for all and take responsibility to help improve things for this student?" Use the chart in Figure 6.2 to begin strategizing your action plan.

Plan to meet again with the student, along with other colleagues, family members, or peers who are included in the success plan. In most cases, you will want to meet weekly to gain momentum around the success plan. Then move to biweekly meetings and finally monthly meetings when the problem begins to settle down.

Figure 6.2: Student Success Plan

Action Steps	Students, Staff, and Support Team	Timetable for Action Steps	Success Milestones

Putting Heartfelt Problem Solving in Action

We've used this process with many students and teams across the country and want to share a few examples in this section to bring our process to life.

Chelsea and the Bracelet

Chelsea was a student who was having difficulty at recess. She would either run from the playground, cry, or get into physical altercations with students, especially when playing tether ball. The teachers and Chelsea's paraprofessional had reached the point of not letting her go out to recess at all because the issues would carry over into the classroom later in the afternoon.

The team sat down together and worked through our problem-solving process plan with Chelsea, her parents, and two of her friends from class, Patrice and Olivia. Although the team came up with many ideas, we have included only the most relevant ones that ended up being successful. The plan entirely changed Chelsea's recess experience.

Step 1. At home on the weekend, Chelsea watches YouTube videos of beading and jewelry design. She loves doing needlepoint and creating pillows.

Step 2. Chelsea is having trouble at recess.

Step 3. Patrice and Olivia asked if it would be OK if they designed jewelry during recess. In the end, the three friends started a jewelry club. They brought a beading set to school and were responsible for managing the materials and supporting other students who wanted to participate. It became so popular that on any given day, there would be 10–15 students sitting with Chelsea in the shade designing jewelry. She seemed to love the responsibility of managing the materials and teaching others about jewelry design. Conversations between students were easy and relaxed.

Step 4. The team, including all three students, used the table in Figure 6.3 to create Chelsea's success plan.

Nico and the Field Trip

Nico was a 9th grade student from Brooklyn, New York, with whom we recently used our problem-solving process. His art teacher, Sarah, had planned a field trip to the Museum of Modern Art, but when she introduced the trip, Nico—a bright kid whom she knew loved art—began screaming and banging his head against his desk. Sarah was confused, so she went up and placed her hand on his shoulder, whispering

Figure 6.3: Student Success Plan in Action

Action Steps	Students, Staff, and Support Team	Timetable for Action Steps	Success Milestones
Buy a beading kit.	Ms. Sol	After school: Monday	Chelsea will let the team know when they receive beads.
Make a poster of the rules for the beads.	Patrice, Chelsea, and Olivia	After school: Tuesday Before school: Wednesday	Ms. Long will provide access to the supplies.
Explain the beads and the rules to the class.	Chelsea reads the poster while Patrice and Olivia hold it.	Morning Meeting: Wednesday	Ms. Long and Ms. Sol will add this item to the Morning Meeting agenda.
Try out the beading activity.	Patrice, Chelsea, Olivia, and fellow classmates	Recess: Wednesday	
Discuss any adjustments for the next day.	Ms. Sol, Patrice, Chelsea, and Olivia	After school: Wednesday	
Revisit this solution with everyone to see if it is still working.	Ms. Sol, Ms. Long, Patrice, Chelsea, and Olivia	Lunch next week: Wednesday	Recess feels more successful for Chelsea.
Patrice, Chelsea, and Olivia will write a note home to all their parents and let them know how it is going.	Patrice, Chelsea, Olivia, and Lea (lunch monitor)	Lunch next week: Thursday	Parents receive notes.

quietly to him, "Nico, hey, you are really upset. Why don't you take some time to calm your body and gather your thoughts. Then later we can talk about how you are feeling."

When Nico was calm, Sarah spoke with him about his emotional response. He told her he was upset because he never went on field trips, but he wouldn't say anything more. Later, Sarah found out that Nico didn't go on field trips because of safety concerns. (He had significant crying and screaming outbursts in middle school and was considered a flight risk during field trips.)

Kate worked with Sarah to plan a problem-solving meeting with her, Nico, and several of Nico's closest friends. We began by identifying and stating the current problem. In the past, Nico had some unsafe behaviors on field trips and had not attended a field trip in over two years. We then asked the group to reframe this problem as a question that could be solved. The group landed on the following question: "How can we help Nico have fun and feel safe and supported on field trips?"

Step 1. We led the group through the process of discovering Nico's strengths. The list was long, but several examples shared were specifically useful in connection to the field trip issue. Nico's teachers and peers noted that he was detail oriented, funny, artistic, and great with directions. He also had an amazing memory.

Step 2. We then took Nico, with the support of his friends, through the process of discovering challenges in relation to field trips. We asked, "What challenges do you face with field trips? What feelings come up for you about these challenges?"

Nico was able to share that he was afraid of many unknowns on a field trip. He worried about what would happen if the train didn't work. What if there was a really loud and long line to get in? He was also able to share that he was mad his fear meant he couldn't go on trips.

We then circled back to the process of discovering strengths and asked, "What currently works to help you with your fear of the unknown?" Nico and his best friend, Tamir, realized Nico had quickly memorized his usual school routes and routines to help him feel comfortable. Nico also always kept a map of the school and the subway lines on him. We wrote strategies for creating clear schedules, keeping consistent routines, and providing maps.

Step 3. We then asked the following questions: "What kinds of support do you need to feel safe on this field trip? How can we use your current strengths, like your excellent memory and attention to detail and direction, to help you succeed?

How can you use your current strategies, like the way you familiarize your school routes and routines using schedules and maps?"

Tamir suggested that he and Nico could take a test-run trip to the museum to get familiar with the train route and museum. Nico shook his head. Another friend, Kayla, suggested that he could map out the best route to get to the museum and the best route for moving through the museum itself to see specific exhibits. Tamir liked this idea and pointed out that they could even include alternative routes, like if the E train was down and they needed to take the A or C train instead.

Step 4. Nico liked the route mapping idea and the alternative plans idea. With these plans as a preferred solution, we led the group through the last step in the process and asked the following questions: "What are our steps? Who will do what? By when? How will we measure success?"

Over the next two weeks, Nico researched the routes. He included the walk to the train, three possible train routes, and how to get around the museum most efficiently. He then used his research findings to create a two-page document that included a visual map of three possible routes from the high school to the museum on one side and a visual layout of the museum on the other side. The museum layout included specific details about the planned exhibits and what to expect at those exhibits.

Another classmate, Kenzie, made copies of Nico's detailed maps for every student on the field trip. Tamir and Kayla made sure Nico knew they would walk with him and sit next to him on the train for support. When the day of the field trip came, Nico was dubbed the unofficial trip leader. He knew exactly how long the estimated train ride would take, which exhibits required waiting in line, and where the gift shop and bathrooms were in relation to the exhibits they planned to see. During the trip, Nico had a few moments where he had to sit down and cover his head with his hands. Nevertheless, when he later reflected on the trip, he said he had a good time and was captivated by the art. He said it was cool that when his peers asked, he knew the fastest path to the bathrooms and gift shop.

Learning the New ABCs

Our examples of heartfelt problem-solving processes in this chapter aren't perfect. Nevertheless, they illustrate many important beliefs about how to effectively and lovingly support students with behaviors that challenge us:

- Including students at the center of the problem-solving process.
- Welcoming student behavior as communication.

- Recognizing that the problem isn't located *within* our students but instead within the way we approach the context, the landscape, and our own responses to behavior.
- Understanding that solutions should increase a student's acceptance, belonging, and connection to community.

Nico and his peers were able to accomplish and experience many things that would never have occurred if he had simply been excused from the field trip. The process created ways for peers to support Nico and for Nico to support his peers. It also created a warm space for Nico, his friends, and the adults in his world to identify his many strengths and some strategies required for support. They worked together to develop ways to build on those strengths and successful support strategies to help him feel safe, successful, and valued by his community.

Chelsea and her peers were also able to accomplish and experience many things that never would have occurred if she had simply been excluded from recess. The process provided a way for Chelsea and her peers to develop a successful plan that would keep her included, which ultimately led to successful gradewide activities that highlighted Chelsea's talents and interests and helped her feel an authentic sense of belonging and connection with her peers.

This heartfelt problem-solving approach can provide opportunities for our students to significantly increase their sense of empowerment and feelings of acceptance, belonging, and community, which decreases challenging behavior and increases needed skills and strategies. The goal of this approach is to help students feel deeply included—safely and meaningfully—in their classroom and school environment.

 **Tiny To-Do List**

- ❏ Practice a heartfelt problem-solving process with a student in mind.
- ❏ Practice the problem-solving process with a colleague.
- ❏ Do something kind for yourself.

Dealing with
Crisis Artfully

The goal of this book is to help students be seen, heard, and supported so they do not end up in an emotional crisis. However, even with thoughtful planning and creative and engaging support for both the student and yourself, some students will still struggle with behavior. In this chapter, we work through steps to implement when a crisis occurs, beginning first by accepting that crises will occur and then figuring out how to respond in compassionate, calm, and loving ways.

Playing the Long Game of Love and Persistence

We were recently in a kindergarten classroom observing Sam, a student with very challenging behavior, and were able to witness a beautiful example of love and connection. As we walked in, Sam was already in a full meltdown. He was screaming, crying, and hitting the carpet with a pillow. It appeared he had already knocked several books off the shelf, as there were many books scattered on the floor, and some looked to be ripped. One of the coteachers had taken the rest of the class to the library a few minutes early in order to help Sam maintain dignity and privacy while the other coteacher stayed behind to support. What we witnessed next was nothing short of magic.

His kindergarten teacher, Mr. Goode, sat on the carpet next to him. He reassured Sam with the following phrases: "I am here. It is going to be okay, I promise."

Sam writhed around screaming and hitting the pillow on the carpet. He was yelling, "I hate you! I hate school! I hate this!" During Sam's outburst, Mr. Goode's disposition remained calm, loving, attentive, nearly meditative. The student sobbed, screamed, and sobbed some more.

Mr. Goode offered, "Do you want my hand on your back?" Sam yelled, "No!" Mr. Goode continued sitting silently next to Sam, breathing slowly, deeply, and audibly. After what seemed like 20 minutes—but was actually only four—something happened. Sam paused and took a shuttering breath and then sighed. Then Mr. Goode said, "There you are."

"There you are," he repeated, as if to say, "I see you now, and you are not your behavior." Sam sighed again and wriggled over to Mr. Goode's leg and rested his head on Mr. Goode's hand. He lay there breathing. Mr. Goode breathed, too. When Sam's breathing finally slowed down and he appeared to be ready to get up, Mr. Goode said, "Let's get a drink of water and wash your face. I am sorry that was so hard for you." They got up to get a drink. Mr. Goode got some water, too. He then said to Sam, "Let's clean up these books and then we can get you to the library." They cleaned up the books together. With Mr. Goode's guidance, Sam taped the book that had ripped. They walked out of the classroom hand in hand.

When Mr. Goode returned, we had a lot of questions for him. The first was "What started this situation?" We learned that Sam had been having a lot of trouble because he only wanted to sit next to a student named Sabrina. But during story time, the two seats next to Sabrina were taken, so Mr. Goode suggested that he find another spot. Mr. Goode then explained, "Sam's rage is big and deep, as you saw. It turned into quite a scene today."

Next, we asked Mr. Goode to tell us exactly what he was doing while sitting on the floor with Sam. Mr. Goode smiled and said, "Well, I am certain none of this can be explained clearly, but I hold space. It may sound strange, but while I sat there, I opened my heart to Sam. I always first make sure the student is safe and I am safe.

"Second, I reassure the student and imagine my heart opening up to him and surrounding him with light. Then I examine my own reactions. I work on calming myself. Again, I know this sounds strange, but I ask myself, 'Where does this hurt?' and 'What does this remind me of?' I send myself love. I surround myself with healing energy. It is fairly traumatizing to witness the pain that some of these children bring. I use it as an opportunity to heal myself, and I know somehow it helps to heal them.

"Next, I listen for the pause. There comes a time with Sam where he moves out of rage and into sadness. I try to let him know he is coming out of it. When I notice the shift, I say, 'There you are.'

"I guess," Mr. Goode continued, "today was a big rage, but it didn't last as long as usual. I am noticing improvement in both the length of Sam's tantrums and also the intensity. After lunch today, we will spend time talking about that situation, at a point when he is calm, but it is still fresh in his mind. That is when I like to teach him alternatives to the rage. He is really improving. It just takes time. Consistency and love are the only real constants in teaching. You just have to be patient enough to see it. This is a long game here."

Although we think Mr. Goode was clear in his explanation, we've outlined his big ideas in Figure 7.1 in an attempt to replicate his calm way of being with a student during a crisis.

This type of response to crisis behavior requires a teacher who is heart-centered and ready to deeply listen to and respond appropriately to the content and context of the student in a rage. Mr. Goode did not react when Sam shouted that he hated him. He did not react when Sam shouted that he hated the class. Instead, Mr. Goode responded by breathing. This is one of the most centering things we can do for ourselves and our students. Although not responding to Sam's shouting could be misinterpreted as planned ignoring (Scheuermann & Hall, 2016), it is not.

The idea behind planned ignoring is to provide no feedback, no attention, no reinforcement to the student. The assumption is that when the teacher withholds

Figure 7.1: Six Steps to Holding Space During Crisis

1. Hold space and open your heart. Visualize your heart opening toward the student.
2. Reassure the student with a few words and imagine the student surrounded with healing light.
3. Examine your own reactions. Ask yourself, "Where does this hurt? What does this remind me of?"
4. Create space to calm and heal yourself.
5. Listen for the pause with your student.
6. Repeat and watch the magic occur over time.

reinforcement or attention related to the behavior (e.g., yelling "I hate you!"), the student will cease to engage in the behavior. Often, when educators use planned ignoring, they do not make eye contact or connect to the student until they are engaged in more appropriate behavior. This is much different from Mr. Goode's continuous and thoughtful connection with Sam. He created space for Sam by physically and emotionally witnessing the crisis, supporting, and providing love. Mr. Goode did not ignore Sam by not reacting. Instead, he provided an attentive response the entire time Sam was in crisis. Mr. Goode did not let Sam's negative statements take him away from his plan to hold space and provide love. This is the goal for supporting students when they're at their most vulnerable.

Staying Safe and Calm

When our students are in crisis, it is important to think about the safety of the student, their peers, and yourself. The best way we can do this is to practice the act of remaining calm. Mr. Goode showed us a great example of what this can look like, as do the six steps for holding space during crisis. By using these six steps (and others we will share in this chapter), you can begin to build calming strength as a critical mental resource to help you stay in the present moment and be ready to work with your students when they are melting down, throwing, kicking, screaming, punching, or self-harming. These are some of the most challenging behaviors that teachers report and that we ourselves have experienced.

We're sure you have heard of the so-called flight, fight, or freeze reactions that biologically occur when we are faced with the threat of emotional or physical pain. Broken down a bit more, psychologist Rick Hanson (Hanson & Hanson, 2018) describes the specific emotional responses in fight, flight, and freeze as fear, anger, and helplessness. These three emotions are present in a great spectrum when we are faced with the threat of emotional or physical pain—uneasiness to panic, annoyance to rage, and feeling overwhelmed to paralysis.

Though it is normal for us to experience these emotions, and as teachers we often feel many combinations of these emotions when we are engaged with a student in crisis, it is critical that we learn and help our students learn to meet these threats of emotional or physical pain with calm strength. When we are calm and present, we can maintain our own emotional and physical state that allows us to utilize all our mental resources to support students most effectively.

Understanding the Science of Crisis

When we feel stress—whether it is emotional, physical, environmental, or academic—our body responds by releasing cortisol. This cortisol then triggers physical reactions, sometimes manifesting in a depleted immune system, increased blood pressure, or tension in large muscles. When our students are stressed and release cortisol, their bodies' physical reactions often result in behavioral outbursts and challenging, difficult-to-manage behavior.

When kids experience high levels of stress and continual high cortisol levels day in and day out, they can begin to react to everyday experiences as if their safety and security is threatened. For example, one student, Tommy, melted into crisis when he was asked to pick up his paper off the ground. This moment of crisis can often feel very confusing for us, but it is important to remember Tommy's physiological response to the various stressors he may be under. His crisis was not a rational, cognitive choice. It was likely a physiological response from continuous exposure to stress throughout his day and life. He also likely did not yet have the skills required to manage his stress and calm his mind and body. Keeping all this in mind is useful as you commit to responding in calm, measured, and reassuring ways when your students are in crisis.

Becoming Mindful of the Breath

When our students are in crisis, our minds and bodies often respond chaotically as we attempt to deal with our emotions, thoughts, body sensations, triggers, and actions all at once. Training ourselves to focus on our breath can help us cultivate a resilience and a calmness that allows us to be present during a student crisis. We can also teach our students this skill to help them come back to themselves from the pain, stress, anger, and powerlessness they are feeling. You can focus on your breath and then invite the student to do the same. We like using hand signals, such as palms up to breathe in and palms down to breathe out. Bringing attention to our breath gives us and the student a chance to move on from flight, fight, or freeze mode—and into recovery mode.

Don't Overestimate Threats or Underestimate Resources

As humans, biologically, we often overestimate a potential threat and underestimate our resources to handle that threat. When a student is crying or screaming, we might overestimate the problem or threat and react as if it were a crisis when in reality, it is not. Have we reflected on our own reaction? Did we breathe deeply? Is the student safe? Can you sit near her and breathe deeply, assuring her that you are there and will wait with her?

Pause and Avoid Speaking or Acting in Anger

This doesn't mean we are asking you to *never* feel anger when a student says something hurtful to you or another student. You might feel anger. This is normal. But we want you to practice not speaking or acting from that anger toward the student. Instead, pause and assess your emotions underneath the anger, such as your concerns or fears. For example, you can say, "I'm angry Joe is calling me hurtful names. Pause. Underneath that anger, I'm concerned because he has disrespected me in front of the class, and I will lose the respect of all the other students if I don't discipline him now."

Once you've acknowledged the anger and its underlying concern, we want you to practice self-compassion and talk to yourself in a heartfelt way. Separate your anger from everything else. Doing these steps will help you stay calm and speak in a way that aligns with the belief that no student is bad—and their behavior is a form of communication.

This is also a practice we can teach our students and colleagues. In many instances, these two steps can help avoid turning challenging behavior into an even greater crisis. For example, take our friend Shane, the assistant principal of a middle school in a small rural district in the northeast United States. One day at her school, a fight broke out between two 8th grade girls. Hair was pulled, faces were slapped and scratched, and yelling echoed through the hallway. Shane was in her office with the principal when the two girls were brought in by a science teacher who had stopped the fight. The teacher began explaining what he had seen. The principal began to order suspensions for both girls while asking who had started the fight and why. In response, the girls started to scream at each other and at the principal.

Shane interrupted and said, "Why don't we all pause?" She paused, took a deep breath, and then continued, "Before we pass blame or suspensions. Let's take some time to cool down and come back together to talk about this when we're not all in such a heated zone." The girls looked at Shane. The principal looked at Shane but then nodded and said to the girls, "Yes, Mrs. Ruddy is right. I'll call your parents to have them come get you today. Tomorrow morning, once we've had time to cool down and think, we'll have a talk to figure out the best consequence and course of action."

We love this example because Shane was able to model the practice of pausing and not acting or speaking from a place of anger or fear for her two students in crisis. After sharing this story with us, Shane reflected on the issues that can arise when adults hastily dole out consequences in the heat of the moment before anyone has had a chance to cool down or discuss what happened. Students feel they are not listened to. They often don't have a chance to attempt a mediation to resolve this issue, and they don't feel connected to the consequence. Instead, Shane likes to pause and come back together when everyone—adults, students, and parents—are calmer and ready to at least attempt to discuss the issue and come to a resolution. When this happens, she says, students feel supported, respected, and listened to.

In this particular crisis at Shane's middle school, the girls did not receive suspensions. Instead, they participated in a mediation session with Shane, who had been formally studying Restorative Practices (RP) and conflict resolution in order to prepare for implementing RP schoolwide the following academic year. Shane, in collaboration with the principal and the two girls, decided that an appropriate consequence for their actions both in harming each other and their 8th grade community hallway would be to provide a service to their peers. They would create a project highlighting the importance of respect and healthy communication between friends and peers.

With the help of their school health teacher, the girls planned a 30-minute lunchtime event for their fellow 8th graders about healthy relationships. This led to an activity about setting boundaries and having clear communication. They shared with their peers that their fight had resulted because of rumors instead of clear communication. Shane was inspired by how effective this approach was to the girls' crisis, how much more the girls learned from mediation and service work in lieu of traditional suspensions, and how it not only helped mitigate the negative impact on the school community but also provided a positive impact.

After dealing with that crisis using RP, Shane was even more committed to implementing the approach schoolwide. Three years later, both her district's middle school and high school use RP as a foundation for supporting all students. Shane reports that in-school and out-of-school suspensions are significantly down, and the attendance and graduation rates at the middle and high schools are up. Her district's positive outcomes are not singular. Research has consistently shown that schools that strive to keep students *in school*—compared with schools that more actively suspend students—have increased student achievement outcomes (Osher, Poirier, Jarjoura, & Brown, 2014).

Creating Your Own Success Plan

In Chapter 6, we outlined our process for heartfelt problem solving that results in developing a success plan for students. Sometimes, though, when crises erupt, we also need to create our own success plan. We recommend using the steps in Figure 7.2 alone or with a friend, colleague, or loved one.

Another important factor in effectively supporting students in crisis is to understand that public reprimands always increase the chance of escalating the student's behavior. Whether it is raising your voice or using a public behavior chart, these types of public displays send a negative message to the student who will then experience a swell of anxiety, embarrassment, and shame. Certainly, we know that students can press our buttons even when we acknowledge and try to always honor these important truths.

Kate vividly remembers during her first month as a teacher, she sent a student named Jonas out of her classroom after getting into an argument about his independent research project.

Jonas had cursed at me and told me he hated me and my stupid class. I remember turning bright red, feeling my flight-or-fight response kicking in, and telling him, "We don't speak to each other like that in here. You better leave now and go to the office to cool down before returning." Oh, did I make a mistake.

At that point in my career, I didn't have the skills to deal with behavior and crisis that I needed. I hadn't committed to understanding that student behavior is communication, and I certainly didn't pause to avoid acting in anger before doling out a consequence. I took everything Jonas said personally. I thought, "He is right; I'm a terrible teacher and my class is stupid!"

Worst of all, I knew I had branded myself as a teacher who sends students out of the room, signaling to Jonas and his peers that he did not belong in our class. This

Figure 7.2: Creating Your Own Student Success Plan

What do I need to recover from this situation?

What might need repair? How can I repair it? What might I need to restore? How can I restore it?

What types of supports can I put in place?

In what ways do I need to fill my cup to be even more prepared for this situation in the future?

What are three steps I can put in place to help me feel more successful?

1.

2.

3.

Is there anyone I need to talk to about this?

was not the teacher I wanted to be, and it was not the teacher Jonas needed me to be. Jonas tested me and instead of leaning in, I pushed back.

When Jonas left my classroom, he didn't come back that period. Or the next day. Or the next. I knew he was skipping class because I made him feel bad, and I had done so in front of his peers. I needed to check in with him and apologize. I needed my own success plan. I sought him out during lunch time in the courtyard where I knew he often hung out with his friends. When I approached the group, he was there but avoided looking at me. I asked if I could speak to him privately and, without speaking, he moved to one side, away from his peers.

I told him that I'd messed up. I shouldn't have raised my voice at him or sent him out of the class. I told him I was sorry I had done it, sorry if I had hurt him, and sorry that even though it hurt my feelings that he had called me names, I was the one who was there to protect him and teach him, and I hadn't done that to the best of my ability. I finished by telling him that I missed him, his humor, and his ideas in class a great deal. I told him I really wanted him to come back to class and figure out how I could help him better—and how he could help himself, too.

He didn't say anything in return, but he came to class the next day. I spent the next few weeks earning his trust back by talking to him quietly; learning more about him, his strengths, and his needs; and leaving him positive and encouraging notes. Jonas was one of my most important early lessons as a teacher. In fact, he helped me determine who I wanted to be as an educator and commit to many of the ideas and strategies discussed in this chapter:

- Practice the pause.
- Avoid acting or speaking in anger.
- Hold a private conversation with the student. Create conversations that maintain their dignity and connect with love, patience, and persistence.

When faced with a student's challenging behavior, imagine you are the parent of that child or someone who loves the child deeply, even if you are still learning to embrace the child, behaviors and all. Consider how you would react from that loving perspective. By reacting from a position of love and acceptance, your response will be with kindness, patience, and humanity—rather than with punishment or control. A crisis response must express compassion for all involved.

Healing with the Arts

Sometimes students aren't able or ready to communicate about pain or suffering. Miranda Field (2016) shows that music, creative writing, performing arts, and fine arts can help calm the body's stress responses and help our students feel safer and calmer in our classrooms. Let's look at a couple examples.

Writing a New Path

Aiden was a student who had been educated full time in self-contained, special education classroom for students with emotional disabilities during 4th grade and part of his 5th grade year. In 5th grade, though, his special education teacher, Kim, and one of the general education teachers in the school, Nancy, wanted to see him included in the general education classroom full time.

Nancy and Kim worked together collaboratively, even shifting Kim's schedule so the two of them could coteach for part of the day in order to provide Aiden and other students with disabilities appropriate services in the general education classroom. With this important collaborative support in place, Nancy and Kim soon realized that Aiden seemed most engaged when writing stories and most energized when playing basketball. They decided that tapping into Aiden's interest in basketball, writing, and stories would be a great way to start building his strengths, show him that they truly believed in his success, and help him identify his feelings and challenges.

Nancy and Kim began by giving Aiden time to write about what he was feeling and experiencing in his life, and when he had freedom to write about his feelings and experiences, he seemed to unlock a whole world. They not only saw the birth of a writer but also witnessed how he began to use written expression to work through some of his own trauma (the death of a grandparent). Over time, his negative behaviors decreased and he was able to make it through an entire school day without any emotional outbursts. Nancy and Kim helped him articulate that he could channel his anger and pain into writing and release some of his anger and pain by playing basketball; thereby, he could be more calming, more soothing, and more loving to himself.

When that school year came to an end, Nancy and Kim wanted to make sure Aiden continued to grow his writing as a powerful coping strategy and creative skill. They encouraged and helped him apply to a summer writing program at The

Telling Room, an organization in their community that supports and empowers youth through writing. Aiden attended the program that summer and continued to hone his writing and even got involved in documentary filmmaking. Later that year, Aiden took part in The Telling Room's community anthology event. He read one of his poems (see Figure 7.3) in front of hundreds of supporters who attended. His teachers were profoundly moved by Aiden's growth as a writer and an empowered communicator of his own trauma—along with the self-compassion and self-understanding he'd learned along the way.

For the Love of Dance

Jane was a 2nd grade student who went into crisis during transitions. Her teacher, Dave, explained, "If she was happy where she was, that's where she wanted to stay. If she was asked to leave that happy place, she'd throw herself onto the floor and kick, scream, and thrash around."

At first, Dave was stumped. He called in the behavior specialist, the special educator, the occupational therapist, and anyone he could get to help figure out Jane's transition crises. During one meeting with the behavior specialist, Trina, Dave explained all the various scenarios in which Jane had been in crisis during transition. Trina looked at him and smiled kindly. She then said, "This question might seem off topic, but I promise it's not. What does Jane love to do?" Dave replied, "I guess she loves to dance. She's actually a terrific dancer." Trina and Dave brainstormed how to incorporate dance into transition time for Jane.

The next day, when Dave asked his class to transition from recess back to class for math, one of Jane's happy places, he told them they would be dancing back to class in a conga line. Jane's face lit up and she beelined to the front of the line in order to lead the conga. When the conga line was such a success, Dave began to brainstorm other types of dancing transitions throughout the day to support Jane. Soon, he realized it would be more fun and collaborative to enlist the help of the entire class. Dave and his students brainstormed a long list of dance transition possibilities, including tangoing with a partner from the desk to the rug for reading (one of our favorites). He hung the list prominently on the classroom wall and referred to it throughout the year to support transition decisions. Dave reflected that although Jane still occasionally struggled with transitions, the dancing was a huge support for her, and his class sure had a lot more fun.

Figure 7.3: Aiden's Poem

MY LIFE

Cancer

took a person I loved

It's hard not getting

to say goodbye

the way I wanted to

I never even got to say the word

It's hard having anger inside

Like a volcano

Ready to erupt a giant rock

that shoots out lava

Smells like ash and fire

breathe me in and you will

suffocate

No one wants a life full of anger

I never wanted a life

Full of anger

I hear my anger

Like a roar of a lion

it gets me mad

My heart pounds with anger

it always pounding

like a drum in me

I feel different than other people

I sometimes feel like I don't belong
  on Earth

No one wants a life full of anger

I never wanted a life

Full of anger

I'm alive when I play basketball

I turn my anger into energy

I get rid of the energy

By playing

basketball

Writing is how

I express my feelings

you can figure out if I'm happy or mad

Hopeful or sad

By reading my writing

the words might have

hate or happiness

I express my feelings through these
  things

Nothing helps but

writing and basketball

Source: Poem by Aiden G. Reprinted with permission.

Following (and Changing) the Plan

Educators often create a crisis plan for any type of emergency, particularly for times when they must react to extremely challenging behavior. Research indicates that a crisis intervention plan offers a coordinated approach for responding to serious incidents (Bender & McLaughlin, 1997; Skiba & Peterson, 2000). Create a crisis binder that includes a note so that in an emergency situation, any adult in charge can follow specific directions for the class. Determine a neutral place where the class could go (e.g., the media center), and have independent work prepared for students. This allows the teacher to be available for an individual student, perhaps simply to sit and breathe together, while maintaining the highest level of safety for the rest of the class in times of crisis.

Although there can be many steps to support a student, sometimes changing those steps is just as important. Simply because you or an entire team has created a fully detailed and scripted crisis plan does not mean you need to stick to it 100 percent of the time. You can decide to change the plan if it will help the student. Just be sure everyone is clear on the changes. Most importantly, be sure the student understands the changes.

There's never a good time to implement a new way to do things in schools, especially if we don't feel ready or if we know it will take a lot of our time and energy to do it well. Nevertheless, if we've learned one thing in our decades of work with educators to create inclusive change, it is this: It will always be too soon.

We were recently inspired by author and entrepreneur Seth Godin (2014), who writes, "There is a fundamental difference between being ready and being prepared. You are more prepared than you realize. You probably aren't ready, and you can't be ready, not if you're doing something worthwhile" (p. 80). Johannes Gutenberg, Godin explains, launched the printing press when 96 percent of the population was illiterate. Karl Benz introduced the car to Germany when it was still against the law to drive one. No one knew how to drive, there weren't roads, and there were no gas stations.

You might not be ready to implement new ways to support kids with challenging behavior, but you are more prepared than you think. Getting started is always worthwhile, especially when you consider that you'll be starting something that will lead to a safer and more loving environment that provides more positive and creative support for your students and for you.

Tiny To-Do List

- ❏ Create your own success plan and have it ready for a crisis.
- ❏ Consider getting students access to artful healing.
- ❏ Write down all the ways you are prepared to do this important work.
- ❏ During a crisis situation, practice the following actions:
    - ❏ Hold space.
    - ❏ Practice pausing.
    - ❏ Breathe.

Proclaiming and Maintaining Loving Spaces

How we care for ourselves is the strongest predictor of how well we can care for others, because we can only give what we have. In order to give love, we must have love of self. In order to be patient with others, we must learn to be patient with ourselves. Our book closes with inspiration and ideas for increasing your happiness and health.

We are so grateful for you. Thank you for spending this time and energy learning with us. We close this book with two proclamations. The first is a reminder that you need to care for yourself. When you can do that, you can create an environment for growth in your classroom. The second is a public declaration of the intention, motives, and aims of a person or group. We view these two proclamations as a series of beliefs that can guide your individual thinking or collective action. If you don't connect to the words we have written, please create your own. Better yet, work with your students to create a shared proclamation. We've provided space for you to do just that.

Reclaiming Our Classrooms as Places of Love: A Teaching Proclamation

I want you to know that when you enter this classroom you are loved.

Here we will treat one another with love and respect.

Every person in here is whole and not broken.

We are here together to help one another shine.

We will not do things perfectly, and that is perfect.

Because imperfection allows us to learn.

I will show up for you each day.

We will show up for one another.

We will be courageous together.

We will be joyful together.

We will have many feelings in here together, and we will learn
how to feel them and support one another.

No matter what, you belong here. Every day and in every way.

Use the space below to write your own classroom proclamation of love:

_____

_____

_____

_____

_____

_____

_____

_____

_____

Declaring Yourself as the Birthplace of Love: A Personal Proclamation

I am the weather maker and deciding factor here today.

I will fill myself up first and keep myself at the center of my work.

I will slow down, breathe, and look to truly see and value each human being in my care.

When I begin to feel overwhelmed, I will stop and check in with myself.

I will drink water, make time to eat, and nourish my body.

I will build connections with colleagues and administrators.

I will acknowledge and celebrate my strengths.

I will show and celebrate the ways I am different.

I will get enough sleep.

I will create and maintain healthy boundaries.

When all else fails, I will slow down and simply be with a student.

All because . . .

I welcome and love all hearts and minds here.

I can create a place where each student belongs.

I choose to see students as whole and complex beings.

I can create a loving place for these beautiful souls.

And I must do it from a place of fullness.

Use the space below to write your own personal proclamation:

_____

_____

_____

_____

_____

_____

_____

_____

_____

12 Practices to Enhance Your Inner Wellness

1. Be present. Teaching requires a moment-to-moment presence. We must stay with the moment and try not to check out or disengage. This is paramount to creating an authentic, emotionally stable relationship with every student in our care. Students learn from our ability to be present with ourselves and with them. Set a timer for 10 minutes. Sit someplace where no one can disturb you. Practice being fully present. Notice every sensation: the breeze, the sun, the color of grass, or a bird. Just be. A daily practice of presence will do so much to support your students.

2. Embody the day. Sit or lie in a comfortable position. Breathe slowly and deeply. Stay with your breath. Start with your feet and pay attention to the sensations of your toes, feet, legs, pelvis, back, stomach, shoulders, and neck. In each place, notice where there is tension or emotion. Gradually release the tension in each area until you reach the tip of your head.

3. Practice "four-five breathing." Breathe in for four seconds. Hold. Breathe out for five seconds. Repeat.

4. Time travel. Albert Einstein once said, "Your imagination is the preview to your life's coming attractions." Call to mind a future goal, such as an upcoming trip, a new car, or a beautiful fruit salad. In your mind, think through all the steps that will bring you to that goal. Take one step toward that goal.

5. Write your tomorrow. On a blank piece of paper, write your great thoughts and intentions about tomorrow. For example, you can write, "I will notice laughter. I will see the beauty in my students. I will be early to school. I will feel refreshed and motivated. I will be awake and alive." Watch these things unfold. It is nothing short of magic. We promise.

6. Reflect on grace. Think of a time when someone offered you grace, especially when you felt you did not deserve it. How did it feel? What might it look like to give a student grace? To forgive them? To see them fully? To think about their whole story. Write a thank-you note to someone for giving you grace. Send it.

7. Write letters of encouragement. Write a letter to a student who is challenging you. Your letter could be created as follows: "I see how hard you are working. I notice all the kind things you said yesterday to your friend. I am so happy you are in my class." Write a positive letter and put it on the student's desk. Keep doing it.

8. Embrace each student "as is." Has anyone loved you exactly for who you were—without wanting to change you? Simply decide that you are not going to change this person and instead love them as they are.

9. Practice being together. So much of our lives is in the doing. A last resort support we would like to put in place is not used very often in schools. It involves taking a student to a new environment or spending quality time together doing something that the student might find enjoyable. These activities could include going for a walk outside, gardening together, going out to lunch, sitting on the swings, practicing yoga, playing a game, or simply drawing together. There is no agenda and nothing but an awakened state of being. The goal here is not to teach but to listen, learn, and be together.

10. Flip your thinking. Write a gratitude list about the student who challenges you the most. What do you love about this person? Is it her smile, her punctuality, the way she challenges you to become better, her creativity, her focus on detail, how strong willed she is, her sense of humor, or her leadership abilities? Keep adding to the list. Make sure they are honest and true. Keep looking for all those incredible gifts.

11. Remember that you are not alone. We know that educators who are happier and more connected to a support network are better able to support their students. Go here to join our large network of educators: www.inclusiveschooling. com. Surround yourself with positive people who will cheer on you and your ideas. Share your stories, share your love, and share your ideas. Build one another up.

12. Just begin. If you wait until you have all the answers, you may never begin. If we ask ourselves, "How can we do this better tomorrow with more love and compassion?" then we can continue to grow, learn, and change the way we work with students whose behavior challenges us. And once you do, the difference you can make in a child's life is immeasurable.

We are so grateful for you. Thank you for reading with us. We hope these practices and ideas support you, your love for teaching, and your love for all the remarkable students who make us better, kinder, more compassionate, and creative teachers.

Tiny To-Do List

❐ Write your own proclamations.

❐ Post your proclamations where you can clearly see them. Read them often.

❐ Select three new practices to try from this chapter.

❐ Share your new practices with a colleague.

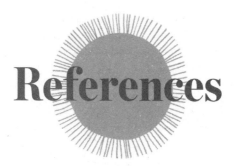

References

Achor, S. (2010). *The happiness advantage: The seven principles of positive psychology that fuel success and performance at work.* New York: Currency.

American Psychological Association Zero Tolerance Task Force. (2008). Are zero tolerance policies effective in the schools?: An evidentiary review and recommendations. *American Psychologist, 63*(9), 852–862.

Aronson, E. (1972). *The social animal.* San Francisco: W. H. Freeman.

Aronson, E. (2000a). *History of the jigsaw.* The Jigsaw Classroom. Retrieved from www.jigsaw.org/history

Aronson, E. (2000b). *A letter from Carlos.* The Jigsaw Classroom. Retrieved from www.jigsaw.org/history/carlos.html

Aronson, E., & Bridgeman, D. (1979). Jigsaw groups and the desegregated classroom: In pursuit of common goals. *Personality and Social Psychology Bulletin, 5*(4), 438–446.

BBC News (2017, May 3) *Seven-year-old returns to school with prosthetic aid.* Retrieved from www.bbc.com/news/av/uk-39797685/seven-year-old-returns-to-school-with-prosthetic-aid

Bender, W. N., & McLaughlin, P. J. (1997). Violence in the classroom: Where we stand. *Intervention in School and Clinic, 32*(4), 196–198.

Bennett, J. (2012). *Levi.* Retrieved from www.youtube.com/watch?v=zoAXfzEU9xU

Benz, M. R., Lindstrom, L., & Yovanoff, P. (2000). Improving graduation and employment outcomes of students with disabilities: Predictive factors and student perspectives. *Exceptional Children, 66,* 509–529.

Boggs, G. L., & Kurashige, S. (2012). *The next American revolution: Sustainable activism for the twenty-first century.* Berkeley, CA: University of California Press.

Brantlinger, E. (1997). Using ideology: Cases of nonrecognition of the politics of research and practice in special education. *Review of Educational Research, 67*(4), 425–459.

Brendtro, L., Brokenleg, M., & Van Bockern, S. (2009). *Reclaiming youth at risk: Our hope for the future.* Bloomington, IN: Solution Tree.

Brown, B. (2010). *The gifts of imperfection: Let go of who you think you are supposed to be and embrace who you are.* Center City, MN: Hazelden.

Carman, K. G., Chandra, A., Miller, C., Trujillo, M. D., Yeung, D., Weilant, S., . . . Acosta, J. (2016). Development of the Robert Wood Johnson Foundation National Survey of Health Attitudes. RAND Corporation.

Carter, E. W., & Hughes, C. (2005). Increasing social interaction among adolescents with intellectual disabilities and their general education peers: Effective interventions. *Research and Practice for Persons with Severe Disabilities, 30*(4), 179–193.

Cartledge, G., Singh, A., & Gibson, L. (2008). Practical behavior-management techniques to close the accessibility gap for students who are culturally and linguistically diverse. *Preventing School Failure: Alternative Education for Children and Youth, 52*(3), 29–38.

Durlak, J. A., Weissberg, R. P., Dymnicki, A. B., Taylor, R. D., & Schellinger, K. B. (2011). The impact of enhancing students' social and emotional learning: A meta-analysis of school-based universal interventions. *Child Development, 82*(1), 405–432.

Epstein, M., Atkins, M., Cullinan, D., Kutash, K., & Weaver, K. (2008). Reducing behavior problems in the elementary school classroom. *IES Practice Guide, 20*(8), 12–22.

Field, M. (2016). Empowering students in the trauma-informed classroom through expressive arts therapy. *in education, 22*(2), 55–71.

Fisher, D., Pumpian, I., & Sax, C. (1998). High school students' attitudes about and recommendations for their peers with significant disabilities. *Journal of the Association for Persons with Severe Handicaps, 23*(3), 272–282.

Fisher, M., & Meyer, L. H. (2002). Development and social competence after two years for students enrolled in inclusive and self-contained educational programs. *Research and Practice for Persons with Severe Disabilities, 27*(3), 165–174.

Froh, J. J., Miller, D. N., & Snyder, S. (2007). Gratitude in children and adolescents: Development, assessment, and school-based intervention. *School Psychology Forum, 2,* 1e13.

Garcia, G. (2017). *Listening with my heart: A story of kindness and self-compassion.* Skinned Knee Publishing.

Godin, S. (2014). *What to do when it's your turn (and it's always your turn).* The Domino Project.

Grant, A. M. (2014). *Give and take: Why helping others drives our success.* New York: Penguin.

Greene, R. W. (2008). *Lost at school: Why our kids with behavioral challenges are falling through the cracks and how we can help them.* New York: Scribner.

Habib, D. (2007). *Including Samuel* [Motion picture]. USA: Pinehurst Pictures and Sound.

Hanson, R., & Hanson, F. (2018). *Resilient: How to grow an unshakable core of calm, strength, and happiness.* New York: Harmony Books.

hooks, b. (2000). *All about love: New visions.* New York: William Morrow.

Howells, K. (2019). The transformative power of gratitude in education. In B. Shelley, K. te Riele, N. Brown, & T. Crellin (Eds.), *Harnessing the transformative power of education* (pp. 180–196). Brill Sense.

Hughes, C., Cosgriff, J. C., Agran, M., & Washington, B. H. (2013). Student self-determination: A preliminary investigation of the role of participation in inclusive settings. *Education and Training in Autism and Developmental Disabilities, 48*(1), 3–17.

Izzo, M. V., & Horne, L. (2016). *Empowering students with hidden disabilities: A path to pride and success.* Baltimore: Paul H. Brookes.

Jones, S. M., & Bouffard, S. M. (2012). Social and emotional learning in schools: From programs to strategies and commentaries. *Social Policy Report, 26*(4), 1–33.

JusTme. (2020). *Mindful moments with JusTme.* Vimeo. Retrieved from https://vimeo.com/yomind

Kluth, P. (2010). *"You're going to love this kid!": Teaching kids with autism in the inclusive classroom* (2nd ed.). Baltimore: Paul H. Brookes.

Kohn, A. (1999). *Punished by rewards: The trouble with gold stars, incentive plans, A's, praise, and other bribes.* Boston: Mariner Books.

Kohn, A. (2006). *Beyond discipline: From compliance to community.* Alexandria, VA: ASCD.

Krajewski, J. J., & Hyde, M. S. (2000). Comparison of teen attitudes toward individuals with mental retardation between 1987 and 1998: Has inclusion made a difference? *Education and Training in Mental Retardation and Developmental Disabilities, 35*(3), 284–293.

Kunc, N. (1992). The need to belong: Rediscovering Maslow's hierarchy of needs. In R. A. Villa, J. S. Thousand, W. Stainback, & S. Stainback (Eds.), *Restructuring for caring and effective education: An administrative guide to creating heterogeneous schools* (pp. 25–39). Baltimore: Paul H. Brookes.

Kurth, J., & Mastergeorge, A. M. (2010). Individual education plan goals and services for adolescents with autism: Impact of age and educational setting. *The Journal of Special Education, 44*(3), 146–160.

Marzano, R. J. (2011). Relating to students: It's what you do that counts. *Educational Leadership, 68*(6), 82–83.

Maslow, A. (1970). *Motivation and personality* (2nd edition). New York: Harper & Row.

Morningstar, M. E., Shogren, K. A., Lee, H., & Born, K. (2015). Preliminary lessons about supporting participation and learning in inclusive classrooms. *Research and Practice for Persons with Severe Disabilities, 40*(3), 192–210.

National Center for Education Statistics. (2019). Student Reports of Bullying: Results from the 2017 School Crime Supplement to the National Crime Victimization Survey. Web Tables. NCES 2017-015. National Center for Education Statistics.

Neff, K. (2003). Self-compassion: An alternative conceptualization of a healthy attitude toward oneself. *Self and Identity, 2*(2), 85–101.

Neff, K. D., & Dahm, K. A. (2014). Self-compassion: what it is, what it does, and how it relates to mindfulness. In I. M. Robinson, B. Meier, & B. Ostafin (Eds.), *Handbook of Mindfulness and self-regulation* (pp. 121–140). New York: Springer.

Neff, K. D., & Germer, C. (2017). Self-compassion and psychological wellbeing. In J. Doty (Ed.), *Oxford handbook of compassion science*. Oxford University Press.

Okonofua, J. A., Paunesku, D., & Walton, G. M. (2016). Brief intervention to encourage empathic discipline cuts suspension rates in half among adolescents. *Proceedings of the National Academy of Sciences, 113*(19), 5221–5226.

Osher, D. M., Poirier, J. M., Jarjoura, G. R., & Brown, R. C. (2014). Avoid quick fixes: Lessons learned from a comprehensive districtwide approach to improve conditions for learning. In D. J. Losen (Ed.), *Closing the school discipline gap: Equitable remedies for excessive exclusion* (pp. 192–206). New York: Teachers College Press.

Quin, D. (2017). Longitudinal and contextual associations between teacher–student relationships and student engagement: A systematic review. *Review of Educational Research, 87*(2), 345–387.

Rosenthal, L., Earnshaw, V. A., Carroll-Scott, A., Henderson, K. E., Peters, S. M., McCaslin, C., Ickovics, J. (2015). Weight- and race-based bullying: Health associations among urban adolescents. *Journal of Health Psychology, 20*(4), 401–412.

Rubin, G. (2009). *The happiness project: Or why I spent a year trying to sing in the morning, clean my closets, fight right, read Aristotle, and generally have more fun*. New York: HarperCollins.

Ryndak, D. L., Alper, S., Hughes, C., & McDonnell, J. (2012). Documenting impact of educational contexts on long-term outcomes for students with significant disabilities. *Education and Training in Autism and Developmental Disabilities*, 127–138.

Sapolsky, R. M. (2017). *Behave: The biology of humans at our best and worst*. New York: Penguin.

Scheuermann, B. K., & Hall, J. A. (2016). *Positive behavioral supports for the classroom* (3rd ed). Upper Saddle River, NJ: Pearson Higher Ed.

Schwartz, I. S., Staub, D., Peck, C. A., & Gallucci, C. (2006). Peer relationships. In M. E. Snell and F. Brown (Eds.), *Instruction of students with severe disabilities* (pp. 375–404). Upper Saddle River, NJ: Pearson.

Shapira, L. B., & Mongrain, M. (2010). The benefits of self-compassion and optimism exercises for individuals vulnerable to depression. *The Journal of Positive Psychology, 5*(5), 377–389.

Shipp, J. (2015). *Like the lap bar on a roller coaster, teens will test you to see if you will hold.* [video] Retrieved from www.youtube.com/watch?v=m51Qf8fc4UA

Skiba, R. J., & Peterson, R. L. (2000). School discipline at a crossroads: From zero tolerance to early response. *Exceptional Children, 66*(3), 335–346.

Skiba, R., & Rausch, M. K. (2006). School disciplinary systems: Alternatives to suspension and expulsion. In G. G. Bear & K. M. Minke (Eds.), *Children's needs III: Development, prevention, and intervention* (pp. 87–102). National Association of School Psychologists.

Soukup, J. H., Wehmeyer, M. L., Bashinski, S. M., & Bovaird, J. A. (2007). Classroom variables and access to the general curriculum for students with disabilities. *Exceptional Children, 74*(1), 101–120.

Test, D. W., Mazzotti, V. L., Mustian, A. L., Fowler, C. H., Kortering, L., & Kohler, P. (2009). Evidence-based secondary transition predictors for improving post school outcomes for students with disabilities. *Career Development for Exceptional Individuals, 32*(3), 160–181.

Tyng, C. M., Amin, H. U., Saad, M. N., & Malik, A. S. (2017). The influences of emotion on learning and memory. *Frontiers in Psychology, 8,* 1454.

Um, E., Plass, J. L., Hayward, E. O., Homer, B. D. (2012). Emotional design in multimedia learning. *Journal of Educational Psychology, 104,* 485–498.

U.S. Department of Education. (2015). 37th Annual Report to Congress on the Implementation of the Individuals with Disabilities Education Act, 2015. Retrieved from https://www2.ed.gov/about/reports/annual/osep/2015/parts-b-c/37th-arc-for-idea.pdf

U.S. Department of Education, Office for Civil Rights (2016). Civil Rights Data Collection, 2015–16. Retrieved from https://www2.ed.gov/about/offices/list/ocr/docs/school-climate-and-safety.pdf

Volkswagen. (2009). The Fun Theory 1: The Piano Staircase. Retrieved from: www.youtube.com/watch?v=SByymar3bds

Watkins, P. C. (2015). *Positive psychology 101.* New York: Springer.

Willis, J. (2007). The neuroscience of joyful education. *Educational Leadership, 64*(9), 1–5.

Zhang, Z., & Chen, W. (2019). A systematic review of the relationship between physical activity and happiness. *Journal of Happiness Studies, 20*(4), 1305–1322.

Index

Page references followed by an italicized *f* indicate information contained in figures.

About the Authors

Julie Causton is founder and CEO of Inclusive Schooling. She is a former professor in the Inclusive and Special Education Program in the Department of Teaching and Leadership at Syracuse University. She has spent the past 20 years studying and creating best practices for inclusive education, with a specific focus on supporting students whose behavior challenges the educational system. As a former special education teacher, she knows firsthand how belonging leads to better outcomes for students. Julie works with administrators, teachers, paraprofessionals, and families across the country to help them create inclusive experiences. She is the author of seven books about inclusive education and has published articles in over 30 educational research and practitioner journals. She lives in Manlius, NY, with her wife, two adorable teenagers, a dog, and three cats. When she is not parenting and working, she enjoys journaling, organizing, and FaceTiming with Kate.

Kate MacLeod is an assistant professor of special education at the University of Maine at Farmington and founder and consultant at Inclusive Schooling. Her teaching, research, writing, and consulting are guided by a passion for inclusive education and social justice. Kate is a former high school special education teacher in New York City and now works with administrators, educators, and families around the country to create more inclusive practices for all students. Her research and writing are focused on understanding the culture of inclusive schools and best practices for supporting students with complex support needs, including those with challenging behaviors. She lives in Maine with her husband, two dogs, a cat, and a flock of chickens. When she is not working, Kate loves to spend time with family and friends, get outdoors, and set new goals with Julie.

Related ASCD Resources: Inclusive Education and Social-Emotional Learning

At the time of publication, the following resources were available (ASCD stock numbers in parentheses). For up-to-date information about ASCD resources, go to www.ascd.org. You can search the complete archives of *Educational Leadership* at www.ascd.org/el.

Print Products

All Learning is Social and Emotional: Helping Students Develop Essential Skills for the Classroom and Beyond by Nancy Frey, Douglas Fisher, and Dominque Smith (#119033)

Brain-Friendly Strategies for the Inclusion Classroom by Judy Willis (#107040)

Creating an Inclusive School, 2nd Edition edited by Richard A. Villa and Jacqueline S. Thousand (#105019)

Engaging Minds in the Classroom: The Surprising Power of Joy by Michael F. Opitz and Michael P. Ford (#113020)

Handling Student Frustrations: How do I help students manage emotions in the classroom? (ASCD Arias) by Renate Caine and Carol McClintic (#SF114068)

Leading an Inclusive School: Access and Success for ALL Students by Richard A. Villa and Jacqueline S. Thousand (#116022)

Self-Regulated Learning for Academic Success: How do I help students manage their thoughts, behaviors, and emotions? (ASCD Arias) by Carrie Germeroth and Crystal Day-Hess (#SF114041)

Teaching in Tandem: Effective Co-Teaching in the Inclusive Classroom by Gloria Lodato Wilson and Joan Blednick (#110029)

What We Say and How We Say It Matter: Teacher Talk That Improves Student Learning and Behavior by Mike Anderson (#119024)

Your Students, My Students, Our Students: Rethinking Equitable and Inclusive Classrooms by Lee Ann Jung, Nancy Frey, Douglas Fisher, and Julie Kroener (#119019)

ASCD myTeachSource®

Download resources from a professional learning platform with hundreds of research-based best practices and tools for your classroom at http://myteachsource.ascd.org/.

For more information, send an e-mail to member@ascd.org; call 1-800-933-2723 or 703-578-9600; send a fax to 703-575-5400; or write to Information Services, ASCD, 1703 N. Beauregard St., Alexandria, VA 22311-1714 USA.

WHOLE CHILD
TENETS

1 HEALTHY
Each student enters school healthy and learns about and practices a healthy lifestyle.

2 SAFE
Each student learns in an environment that is physically and emotionally safe for students and adults.

3 ENGAGED
Each student is actively engaged in learning and is connected to the school and broader community.

4 SUPPORTED
Each student has access to personalized learning and is supported by qualified, caring adults.

5 CHALLENGED
Each student is challenged academically and prepared for success in college or further study and for employment and participation in a global environment.

THE WHOLE CHILD

The ASCD Whole Child approach is an effort to transition from a focus on narrowly defined academic achievement to one that promotes the long-term development and success of all children. Through this approach, ASCD supports educators, families, community members, and policymakers as they move from a vision about educating the whole child to sustainable, collaborative actions.

From Behaving to Belonging relates to the **supported**, **safe**, and **engaged** tenets.
For more about the ASCD Whole Child approach, visit **www.ascd.org/wholechild.**